Camping and Caravanning in France
The "Survival" Guide

by

Rick Allen

Editions
de la
Montagne

Editions
de la
Montagne

PO Box 732
Southampton
SO16 7RQ
England

Published by Editions de la Montagne

ISBN 0 9533386 0 6

Origination by Zip Imagesetters Ltd., Southampton
Printed by Hobbs the Printers Ltd., Totton, Hampshire

Acknowledgements

The Author would like to thank the following for their invaluable help
and encouragement without which this book would not have been written:

Michel Gouvenou
Stéphanie Gouvenou
Marilyn Jamieson
Jacques Moncuit
Philippe Salers
Danielle Volders
Véronique Volders

Simon Carter

Special appreciation is due to Paddy, for her dedication to this project as well as her patience and
hard work in retyping the text.

RJA

This book is dedicated to the memory of Jean-Jacques

Ami, Campeur

Table of Contents

8

Banks - Credit cards - Shopping - Conversion charts - Clothes sizes
- Hairdressing

9

Public telephones - Cheap rates - Phone cards - Tourist Offices
- Bank Holidays - Sanisettes - Post Office

Note:-

Abbreviations in the vocabulary:

        ms = masculine singular i.e. **le** or **un**

        fs = feminine singular i.e. **la** or **une**

        mpl / fpl = masculine / feminine plural i.e. **les** or **des**

1

Before you go!

There are over 3400 Tourist Offices in France, many of them in very small towns / villages. They can supply much more specific and detailed literature than may be obtained from the **Maison de la France** in London. Just write to the **Syndicat d'Initiatives / Office du Tourisme** of the town, requesting brochures etc. See draft letter.

Useful addresses

Maison de la France
178, Piccadilly
London W1V 0AL

Tel: (0891) 244123

Paris Tourist Office
127 Champs-Elysées
75008 Paris

Tel: 01 49 52 53 54
Fax: 01 49 52 53 20
Open daily 9am-8pm except 1st May

Camping and Caravanning Club

Greenfields House
Westwood Way
Coventry
CV4 8JH

Tel: (01203) 856797
Fax: (01203) 694886

The Caravan Club

East Grinstead House
East Grinstead
West Sussex
RH19 1UA

Tel: (01342) 326944 - General Enquiries:
Tel: (01342) 316101 - Travel Service
                                          Reservations
Tel: (01342) 327410 - Travel Service Brochure
                                          Requests

Fédération Française de Camping et de Caravaning
78, Rue de Rivoli
75004
Paris

Tel: 01 42 72 84 08
Fax: 01 42 72 70 21

The FFCC produces an excellent annual guide to campsites - over 11,000 classified locations, - the **"Guide Officiel Camping Caravaning"** including **Camping à la Ferme** (Farm Sites). It is obtainable by post or in person from the Rue de Rivoli - the staff are helpful and speak English. This Guide can also be found in large bookshops in France.

The **Guide Michelin** (English Edition) sold in the UK, is another excellent source of campsite information, but it gives only a selection of sites whereas the FFCC Guide lists them all. Note also that only Michelin sites are marked on its own maps. The **Guide** sets its own independent standards, represented by 1-5 tents.

The Caravan Club's Continental Sites Guide and Handbook is also very good and is based on members' ongoing assessments. It is on sale to non-members as well.

Most municipalities run their own sites, often at a subsidized cost. Each site is star rated (1 étoile - 5 étoiles) by the local **Préfecture** according to strict national standards.

Many sites but by no means all will accept advance bookings. Most will require a deposit. You can use the appropriate draft letter - see the following pages.

When writing to a French address, enclose an International Reply Coupon, obtainable from UK post offices - this enables the other person to reply at no cost. You may well not get a reply if you do not!

Draft Letters

Letter to Tourist Office (Syndicat d'Initiatives / Office du Tourisme)

Name
Address

Monsieur / Madame,

J'envisage de passer mes vacances d'été en France, au mois de *juin / *juillet / *août. Je vous serais reconnaissant de bien vouloir m'envoyer des dépliants sur la région de ... / sur la ville de ... , y compris un plan de la ville. Je voudrais aussi *une liste des campings départementaux / *une liste des hôtels / *une liste des chambres d'hôte / *le programme des manifestations d'été / *une fiche horaire des trains pour ...

Veuillez agréer, Monsieur / Madame, mes salutations distinguées,

(Signature)

PJ: Coupon-Réponse International

(*Change/delete as appropriate)

Letter to Tourist Office - Translation

Dear Sir / Madam,

I intend to spend my Summer holidays in France in *June / *July / *August. I would be grateful if you would kindly send me brochures on the region of ... / *on the town of ... , including a town map. I would also like *a list of Departmental Campsites / * a list of hotels / *a list of Bed and Breakfast establishments / * the local entertainment summer programme / * a train timetable for ...

Yours faithfully,

(Signature)

Enc: International Reply Coupon

If you are travelling to a Camping Holiday where everything is provided, you may need to book an hotel for a night's transit accommodation.

Booking an Hotel

Specimen Letter

A. Camper
"Al Fresco"
21, Canvas Green
Wetfield in the Marsh
OU1 2DC
Grande Bretagne
le 28 janvier 1999

Hôtel Concorde
Place de Verdun
23 100 Guéret
France

Monsieur / Madame,

Je voudrais retenir une chambre pour ... personne(s) / *avec petit déjeuner / *salle de bains / *douche pour deux* nuits, les *5 ... et *26 ... *juin / *juillet / *août prochains. Je vous serais reconnaissant de bien vouloir me faire savoir par retour du courrier si vous avez une chambre de libre pour ces dates et de m'indiquer le montant des arrhes que je dois verser. Je confirme ainsi ma réservation et vous prie de me garder la chambre jusqu'à une heure tardive si besoin est. Sauf imprévu, j'arriverai dans l'après-midi / en début de soirée.

Veuillez agréer, Monsieur / Madame, mes salutations distingués.

A. Camper

PJ: Coupon-Réponse International

(* Change/delete as appropriate)

See also classified phrases for variations on the above

Booking an Hotel - Translation

Dear Sir / Madam,

I would like to book a room for ... person(s) *with breakfast / *bathroom / *shower / for two* nights, the *5th and *26th *June / *July / *August 1998. Would you kindly let me know by return if you have a room available for these dates and the amount of deposit required. Please accept this letter as a firm booking. I would ask you to retain the room until late if necessary but we expect to arrive in the afternoon / early evening.

Yours faithfully,

A. Camper

Enc: International Reply Coupon

Booking your Campsite

Booking Form - Photocopy if you wish and fill in with your personal requirements as appropriate.

Nom ....

Prénom(s) ....

Adresse

.... Rue

.... Ville

.... Département

.... Code Postal

Grande Bretagne

Monsieur / Madame,

Je voudrais retenir un emplacement pour:

.... camping-car(s)
.... caravane(s)
.... tente(s)
.... adulte(s)
.... enfant(s) dont ..... moins de 7 ans

du   / /   au   / /   inclus (.... nuitées)

Je confirme ainsi ma réservation et vous prie de me garder l'emplacement jusqu'à une heure tardive si besoin est. Sauf imprévu, *nous arriverons / *j'arriverai *dans l'après-midi / *en début de soirée. Je vous serais reconnaissant de bien vouloir me communiquer par retour du courrier vos tarifs et le montant des arrhes que je dois verser pour la réservation.

Veuillez agréer Monsieur / Madame, mes salutations distinguées

(Signature) ....   PJ: Coupon-Réponse International

6

Booking Form - Campsite - Translation

Surname   ....

First name(s)   ....

Home Address

....   Street

....   Town

....   County

....   Post Code

Great Britain

Dear Sir / Madam,

I wish to book a site for:

           ....   motor-caravan(s)

           ....   caravans

           ....   tent(s)

           ....   adult(s)

           ....   child(ren) ..... under 7 years

from   /   /   to   /   /   inclusive (.... nights)

Please accept this as a firm booking. I would ask you to keep the pitch free until late if needs be, but *we / *I expect to arrive *in the afternoon / *early evening if all goes well. I would be grateful if you would kindly send me by return a copy of your charges, including the amount of deposit you require for this reservation.

Yours faithfully,

..........................(signature)   Enc: International Reply Coupon

Hotel / Campsite Cancellation / Booking amendment

> A. Camper
> "Al Fresco"
> 21, Canvas Green
> Wetfield in the Marsh
> OU1 2DC
> Grande Bretagne
>
> le 15 mai 1999

Hôtel Concorde
Place de Verdun
23 100 Guéret
France

Monsieur / Madame,

Pour des raisons indépendantes de ma volonté *je suis contraint d'annuler la réservation que j'avais faite pour le *3 juin / *Je me vois obligé de vous demander de reporter ma réservation du *3 juin au *18 juillet. J'espère que ce changement ne vous causera pas de problèmes.

Veuillez agréer, Monsieur / Madame, mes salutations distingués.

A. Camper

PJ: Coupon-Réponse International

(* Change/delete as appropriate)

8

Hotel / Campsite Cancellation / Booking amendment - Translation

A. Camper
"Al Fresco"
21, Canvas Green
Wetfield in the Marsh
OU1 2DC
U K

15th May 1999

Hôtel Concorde
Place de Verdun
23 100 Guéret
France

Dear Sir / Madam,

For unavoidable reasons I am obliged to *cancel my booking for the 3rd June / *I have to request that you change my booking from the *3rd June to the *18th July. I apologize for any possible inconvenience.

Yours faithfully,

A. Camper

Enc: International Reply Coupon

Regional UK Passport Offices

Belfast Passport Office
Hampton House
47-53 High Street
Belfast BTI 2QS
Tel: (01232) 232371

Newport Passport Office
Olympia House
Upper Dock Street
Newport
Gwent NP9 I XA
Tel: (01633) 244500

London Passport Office
Clive House
70 Petty France
London SW1 H 9HD
Tel: (0171) 799 2290

Liverpool Passport Office
5th Floor
India Buildings
Water Street
Liverpool L2 0QZ
Tel: (0151) 237 3010

Glasgow Passport Office
3 Northgate
96 Milton Street
Cowcaddells
Glasgow G4 0BT
Tel: (0141) 332 0271

Check List

(Not for the fainthearted or the Backpacker)

Bank

Calculator
Cheque book
Credit cards
Currency
Eurocheque card
Eurocheques
Travellers' cheques

Bedding

Airbeds
Blankets
Camping beds / mats
Duvets
Pillows
Sheets
Sleeping bag liners
Sleeping bags

Car

Bulbs (spare set)
Fire extinguisher
Fuses (spare)
GB Sticker
Handbook
Headlight converters
Jack
Jump leads
Keys
Mirrors (extensions)
Picnic stools / table
Tools
Towball cover
Towrope
Warning triangle
Wheel (spare)
Wheelbrace

Caravan / tent

Awning
Bucket (toilet)
Bucket (water)
Car hookup lead (car to caravan / tent)
Caravan keys
Chain and padlock
Chairs
Chemical toilet
Chemical toilet additive
Chocks
Clothes line and pegs
Cooker / ring
Corner pads
Damper / handle
Fire blanket
Fire extinguisher
Gas bottle and refills
Gas lamp
Gas regulator
Gas washers
Groundsheet
Hitchlock
Inflator
Levellers
Mains lead
Nose weight gauge
Peg mallet
Spare wheel
Spirit level
Step
Tent
Tent pegs
Toilet rolls
Toilet tent
Tools
TV aerial
TV aerial leads
TV aerial pole

11

TV and power cords
Washing up bowl
Waste containers
Water bottle
Water container
Water filter
Water hose + attachments
Wheel clamp
Wheelbrace
Winder

Cleaning

Bleach
Detergent
Disinfectant
Dustpan + brush
Kitchen cloths
Rubber gloves
Rubbish bags
Surface cleaner
Tea towels
Washing up liquid

Clothing

Anoraks
Clothes
Coathangers
Money belt
Night wear
Shoes (walking)
Socks
Sunglasses
Sunhats
Swimming gear
Towels - bath / hand
Track suit
Underwear
Waterproofs
Wellies

Cooking

Aluminium foil
Barbecue

Bottle opener / corkscrew
Bread knife
Butter dish
Charcoal
Chopping board
Coffee filter / papers
Coolbox
Crockery
Cruet
Cutlery
Firelighters
Food
Frying pan
Glasses (wine)
Ice pack
Kettle
Kitchen roll
Matches
Mess tins
Mugs (plastic)
Oven glove
Pressure cooker
Sandwich bags
Sandwich / salad boxes
Saucepans
Teapot
Tin opener
Vacuum flasks

Medical

Antihistamine cream
Antiseptic / antiseptic cream
Diarrhoea tablets
Headache remedy
Insect repellent
Plasters
Prescription medicines
Suntan oil
Travel sickness tablets
Wasp sting spray

Toiletries

Electric razor
Hairdryer

Handwipes
Heated curlers
Makeup
Nail scissors
Shampoo
Shaving kit
Soap
Toilet bags
Toothpaste / brushes

Miscellaneous

Alarm clock
Batteries
Binoculars
Beach mats
Boules
Compass
Flyspray
Lighters
Map measure
Penknife
Spectacles
Sunglasses
Torch / batteries
Umbrella
Walking stick

Travel documents / paperwork

Address book
Atlas
"Camping and Caravanning in France"!
Camping carnet - essential on some sites - provides
public liability insurance and protection against non payment
for site owner.
Camping guides
Club site book
Dictionary
Driving licence (International Driving Licence not required)
E 111 (See also Section 6 - Refunds)
Ferry timetables
First Aid book
Green Card
Insurance (holiday, sickness, car, breakdown)
List of car dealers in holiday area

Log book
Maps / Map case
Membership cards
Passport
Note of all essential telephone numbers including credit card cancellation
Separate note of Travellers' Cheque and Eurocheque serial numbers
Photocopies of passport and other essential documents
Phrase book
Tickets
Travel guides

Video / still camera

Still camera and films
Tripod
Video batteries / charger / discharger
Video camera
Video light
Video remote
Video tapes

Before departure

Arrange care of pets
Cancel all deliveries
Inform Neighbourhood Watch
Leave key with neighbour
Lock doors / close windows
Turn off gas / water / electricity

Car checks

Battery level
Car oil level
Lights
Roof rack / box
Water level
Tyre pressures

Caravan / Trailer Checks

Brake off
Caravan windows shut / door locked
Caravan / Trailer Lights
Coupling secure
Jockey wheel up

Keys
Legs up
Noseweight
Rooflight closed
Tyre pressure

You may feel that it is sensible to take supplies of certain consumables with you because of:

- Cost

- Difficulty in obtaining familiar brands of such things as proprietary medicines, diabetic and hygiene products, baby food, toiletries, cereals etc

Calor Gas is not obtainable on the continent. Refilling of the cylinders by other companies is highly dangerous and should never be done.

If you intend to travel regularly or for an extended period either:

- Take extra supplies

- Use Camping Gaz (very expensive)

- Buy a 13Kg cylinder of **Butagaz** or **Totalgaz** or similar - on sale at French Filling Stations. The regulators are the same for every brand (apart from Camping Gaz) and are readily available in supermarkets. The pressure is compatible. The cost per kilo of these brands is about half the UK equivalent and the cylinder can be simply returned at the end of the trip to any garage outlet selling the particular brand for a refund of the deposit. The disadvantage is of course that no credit is given for unused gas.

- New 6Kg cylinders of butane and 5 Kg propane were introduced in 1998 by Butagaz (le Cube), Total (Malice) and Primagaz (Twiny). Special clip-on regulators are on sale at the gas retailers, e.g. garages.

As a rough guide, gas appliances use about the amounts shown:

Appliance	Butane kg/hr	Propane kg/hr
Cooker	0.60	0.55
Hotplate / grill	0.52	0.50
Space Heater	0.12	0.13
Refrigerator	0.017	0.018
Instant water heater	0.82	0.82

Travel Tips

Payment of travel fares by credit card will often provide varying degrees of insurance (usually only accident) cover whilst travelling - Free! Check with your company.

Make sure you have adequate personal travel and health insurance as well as carrying the E111. You may be prepared to risk your worldly possessions, but for medical emergencies the reciprocal health arrangements between France and the UK represented by the E111 do not cover 100% of costs of medical treatment. (See relevant pages).

If you are not a member of a motoring organization such as the AA, Green Flag or RAC, do make sure you have adequate insurance to cover repatriation of your vehicle and hire of a replacement in the event of damage. Not only is the cost very high but the arrangements difficult and time-consuming. Thousands of UK motorists break down in France every year, many on the first day! 10,000 AA members alone!

It is a good idea to take and keep separately in a safe place (photo)copies of:

- Passport

- Eurocheque numbers

- Telephone numbers

- Car Registration Document (Log Book)

- Credit Card numbers (not the PIN!)

- Telephone number for reporting card loss

- Insurance Documents (Health and Baggage)

If you have trouble remembering credit card numbers, use a pin safe square:
Say your PIN no is 3451, choose a word of the same number of letters that is easy to recall eg "pink" and write each number of your PIN below one of the letters that spells it:

A	B	C	D	E	F	G
1	7	9	9	4	2	1
H	I	J	K	L	M	N
5	4	5	1	3	7	5
O	P	Q	R	S	T	U
1	3	8	7	4	9	6
V	W	X	Y	Z		
8	4	2	1	1		

Now complete it by filling in all the other numbers at random as shown above.

Customs and Excise

- You no longer need to make any declaration to Customs unless you have any prohibited or restricted items or excess quantities of otherwise allowable goods eg Beer. (See Guide Levels below)

- You may not see Customs when you arrive in the UK or France but selective checks **may** still be carried out.

- Provided they are for your personal use there is no further tax to be paid on goods you have obtained in the European Community.

- Personal use includes gifts, but if you are receiving any payment in return for buying alcohol and tobacco (such as help with travelling expenses) the transaction will be dutiable and you should contact HM Customs and Excise to arrange to pay the duty owed.

- If you bring more than the amounts in the guide levels you must be able to show that the goods are for your personal use.

The guide levels are:

Cigarettes	800
Cigarillos	400
Cigars	200
Smoking tobacco	1Kg
Spirits	10 litres
Intermediate products (such as port and sherry)	20 litres
Wine	90 litres (of which not more than 6 litres sparkling)
Beer	110 litres

Vin de Pays de l'Hérault

Product de France
Mis en bouteille par FDL à F-34200 FRAMECO
Au Pays des Vignes   11% vol.
75 cl

- Never carry anything into another country for somebody else.

- Don't take prohibited goods.

- Motorists: make sure that everyone travelling with you knows what is prohibited or restricted, **including animals and plants. (Plants may be subject to CITES (Convention on International Trade in Endangered Species) controls if they are considered to be of an endangered species.**

- **Otherwise Travellers returning from EU countries are allowed concessions: it is permitted to bring back any plant so long as it was grown in the EU and is:**

    - In your personal luggage

    - For your own household use and not intended for use in the course of business

- Free from signs of disease and pests.

- If you are in doubt go to the Customs enquiry point.

- If you smuggle goods or animals in a car, the car may be confiscated. Other severe penalties can be imposed on anyone breaking customs regulations, including unlimited fines and up to a year's imprisonment for deliberate contravention of Anti-Rabies regulations.

- You must declare any goods in excess of the allowances, restricted or prohibited items. Go to the Red Point or into the Red Channel.

- **Only** go through the Green "Nothing to Declare" channel if you are sure that you have no more than the Customs allowances and no prohibited or restricted goods.

Duty free allowances

Still table wine	2 litres
and	
Spirits or strong liqueurs over 22% volume	1 litre
or	
Fortified or sparkling wine, other liqueurs	2 litres
Cigarettes	200
or	
Cigarillos	100
or	
Cigars	50
or	
Tobacco	250 grams
Perfume	60 cc/ml
and	
Toilet Water	250 cc/ml

- Duty free allowance on each single journey.

- Adult passengers only are entitled to tobacco or drinks allowance.

Regulations now allow you to bring back twice as much Duty Free as previously i.e. one allowance on both outward and return journeys.

These are still applicable but are due to end 30th June 1999.

2

Boats and trains and planes …

Channel Crossings

Ferry Company Reservations

Brittany Ferries

Plymouth	Tel:	(01752) 263388
Portsmouth	Tel:	(01705) 751833
Truckline	Tel:	(0990) 360360
Holyman Sally Ferries	Tel:	(0990) 595522
Hoverspeed	Tel:	(0990) 240241
Sea France	Tel:	(0990) 711711
P&O European Ferries	Tel:	(0990) 980555

The Channel Tunnel

Road Travel Times from Shuttle Terminal		
Destination		
Miles from Shuttle		**Time from Terminal**
Amiens	87	$2^{1/2}$ hrs
Arras	68	$1^{1/2}$ hrs
Boulogne	20	$^{1/2}$ hr
Lille	70	$1^{3/4}$ hrs
Paris	175	$3^{1/2}$ hrs
Reims	168	$3^{1/2}$ hrs
Rouen	130	$2^{1/2}$ hrs

Le Shuttle and Eurostar

Folkestone - Calais - Turn up and go!

- 60 minutes from motorway to motorway 35 minutes from platform to platform

- Up to 4 departures per hour in daytime and a minimum of 1 departure per 75 minutes at night. Some night crossings may take an extra 10 minutes

- 365 days per year, 24 hours per day without reservation for cars - just buy your ticket at the toll booth when you exit the M20 at junction 11A. Toll booth staff will tell you when the next departure is due. You can either leave on the first available train or spend time in the duty free shops or just relax. There are no Duty Free facilities aboard the train! A certain number of spaces is always reserved for Turn-Up-And-Go passengers

- Passport and random Customs checks are completed before departure

- Motorcycles, campervans and cars towing caravans or trailers must be booked in advance

- Tickets purchased within 7 days of travel will be available at the Le Shuttle tolls at Junction 11A on the M20. Quote your eight digit reference number

- There are toilets on board

- It is advised that you arrive at least 25 minutes (and no more than 2 hours) before departure time

- Channel Travel Radio on 107.6 FM keeps you updated as you drive on the M20

- Radio Le Shuttle broadcasts music and travel news -   English 99.8 FM
                                                          French 95.6 FM

Passenger Bookings: Tel: (0990) 353535

The camping clubs and the motoring organizations also book crossings and offer discounts for members.

Remember! You are not allowed to carry fuel jerricans, full or empty, on ferries or Le Shuttle.

Airlines

Air France   Tel: (0181) 742 3377

AirUK   Tel: (0345) 666777

British Airways   Tel: (0345) 222111

Aurigny   Tel: (01703) 612829

Train Travel

Onward travel from one of the Channel ports will often involve going via Paris as the main lines tend to radiate from the capital.

SNCF Stations Paris

SNCF (Headquarters)
88, rue St Lazare, Paris 9e
Tel: 01 42 85 60 00

Gare d'Austerlitz
55, quai d'Austerlitz, 13e

Gare du Nord
18, rue de Dunkerque, 10e

Gare de Bercy
48 bis, boulevard de Bercy, 12e

Gare de Paris-Lyon
pl. Louis Armand, 12e

Gare de l'Est
pl. du 11 Novembre 1918, 10e

Gare de Paris-Vaugirard
rue du Cotentin, 15e

Gare Montparnasse
16-24, pl. Raoul Dautry, 15e

Gare St-Lazare
rue St-Lazare, 8e

Rail Information

Information - All Stations	Tel: 01 45 82 50 50
Booking all stations and Motorail	Tel: 01 45 65 60 60
Timetable and Fare information - Ile de France	Tel: 01 45 65 60 00
Information and Bookings	Tel: 01 45 82 50 50

Timetables and Bookings
Minitel: 3615 SNCF

French trains

Travel by train in France is an
altogether different experience
from in Britain. Massive
investment in all sectors of the
network has ensured a modern,
fast, safe, reliable and punctual
service.

Sample Journey Times by TGV (Train Grande Vitesse)

Paris	Montélimar	2hrs 45 mins
	Avignon	3hrs 45 mins
	Marseille	5hrs
	Toulon	5hrs 45 mins
Lille	Lyon	3hrs 30 mins
	Montpellier	6hrs 30 mins

Booking procedures

TGV: Advance booking is obligatory for ALL journeys. It may be done up to two months before departure.

How to do it:

At a UK Travel Agent whilst you are still in the UK.

When in France:

- By telephone: Just phone the Information and Telesales Centre to book your seat. Ticket issue:
  Paris: Tel: 01 45 82 50 50

- Other Departments: Look in the **Guide du Voyageur** (obtainable from railway stations' leaflet stands) under **Centres d'Information et de Vente par Téléphone.**

- It is advisable to make a note of your travel reference number at the time of booking as well as the time limits for collection of your ticket. All tickets not drawn within these limits will be cancelled automatically.

- Last minute reservations: Use either the many automatic machines or station Ticket Offices. If available, seats may be booked on the next TGV.

- **Note**: Some tickets may be sold "subject to seat being available". These permit access to the train but do not guarantee a seat. The Ticket Collector will endeavour to find a seat for you.

- **Changes of plan**: You can change your travel plans right up to the departure of your TGV. Tickets are exchanged free of charge for other dates or times in automatic machines for a same day departure or at Ticket Offices. Fare differences will be charged / refunded as appropriate.

- Last minute tickets should be purchased at the "**Départ Immédiat**" kiosk.

- Your ticket may be checked on the platform. Have it ready to show.

- Before getting on the train, validate your ticket in one of the red machines at the barrier. Push in the ticket and slide to the left. This validation is most important and must be done on both the outward and return legs at each time of travel if the ticket is a Return. Validation sets a time limit on the usage of the ticket. Travel in respect of the validated leg must take place before midnight the next day.

- If you have not had time to buy, or have forgotten to validate, your ticket, speak to the Ticket Collector at the first opportunity. He will issue a ticket at a special (slightly higher) "on board" rate. If you do not do so and are caught, there is a fixed penalty depending on the circumstances.

- Payment on board the train is only by cheque or in cash.

Cancellations

- Refunds may be made at any Ticket Office unless the ticket was issued by a Travel Agent, in which case, application must be made to the same agency.

- Within an hour of departure, 10% of the ticket price is deducted. Unused tickets are refundable up to two months from reservation date. Refunds are not allowed on part-used tickets.

- Some tariffs are subject to special refund conditions.

On board facilities

Restaurant Service First Class: On most TGV with journey times over an hour. Menus are frequently changed for the benefit of regular travellers. Reserved in advance, meals are cheaper and you are sure of being served. Meal reservations are valid only for the train for which they are booked.

Bar Service: Non-Smoking: Serves quick meals, snacks, hot drinks and the usual range of alcoholic beverages. Also sold are phone cards and magazines. The bar is situated between First and Second Class.

Telephone: On most TGV's. World-wide calls possible.

Luggage: Luggage racks are above the seats or at the ends of compartments for heavier items. Do not leave valuables unsupervised. Trolleys are available in many stations, some requiring a returnable deposit as in supermarkets.

Other services:

Luggage Registration: Heavy / bulky items may be registered.

Left Luggage: Both automatic and manned in the larger stations.

Peak / Off Peak Travel

On the TGV, there are four ticket prices for each class of travel. The **Calendrier Voyageurs** does not apply.

Prices are of course based on time and date of travel:

Category 1	TGVs with seats available in 1st and 2nd class
Category 2	TGVs which are much in demand in 1st class but less so in 2nd
Category 3	TGVs which are much in demand in 2nd class but less so in 1st
Category 4	TGVs which are in great demand in both classes

On trains other than the TGV, booking is sometimes advisable but not usually compulsory. A **Calendrier Voyageurs** also operates. This is published for Oct-Mar and April-September and is easily available from timetable display racks in stations. The BLUE and WHITE periods correspond to the OFF-PEAK and PEAK periods for which different fares are charged. TGV journeys are subject to their own four fare scales as above, not those dictated by the Calendrier Voyageurs.

In general, travel on Saturdays after 12h00, Sundays up to 15h00, Mondays after 12h00 and until 12h00 on Fridays is cheaper and less crowded. Eves of public Holidays and the immediate aftermath are of course Peak Periods. Use of the **Carte Orange** is however unrestricted (except in terms of the number of zones opted for on purchase) as regards time or indeed class of travel.

Calendrier Voyageurs - Typical weekend until 31st May for example.

V = Friday
S = Saturday
D = Sunday
L = Monday

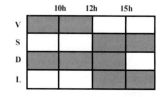

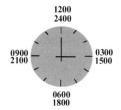

24 Hour Clock

This is in use for timetables and frequently in speech.

Many French trains have names as well as numbers, eg **Sven**. This name is used by every train on a particular route, thus making it easy to verify at a glance whether the train is in fact the required one.

Carte Orange

For anyone staying in or near Paris for a few days, the **Carte Orange** is an excellent investment.

The weekly ticket (**Carte Orange Hebdomadaire**) is purchased at **SNCF** (French Railway) stations. A passport size photo must be affixed to the card, although ticket clerks will inform you that it is not required

for a weekly ticket provided you are carrying ID! (Putting this to the test could prove expensive though if one met a difficult **contrôleur!**) A self-adhesive laminate is then put over the front. The card number must be written on the (renewable) "**coupon hebdomadaire**" which resembles a **Métro** ticket. Once equipped with this card, the traveller can use any public transport (buses, trams, trains, **Métro**) within the (requested and paid for) eight designated zones of the Paris area. It is on sale from Friday midday for the following week. Its

convenience and value cannot be over-emphasized. DO NOT HOWEVER PUT IT IN THE TICKET VALIDATION MACHINES ON BUSES OR AT RAILWAY STATIONS. IT WILL IMMEDIATELY BE CANCELLED! It must though be used like an ordinary Métro ticket for access to the underground and the **RER**. In the Métro Stations, connections to other lines, as well as **SNCF** Main Line Stations and the **RER** are indicated by the orange sign **CORRESPONDANCE**.

- Single **Métro** / bus tickets or books (carnets) of ten tickets (much cheaper) are on sale at authorized agents showing the green sign.

- Children 4-10 years travel half price.

- 1 ticket is sufficient for any journey in Paris by either **Métro** or bus. In the outskirts, a maximum of 2 tickets is required.

- A ticket purchased in the suburbs to a Paris Railway station includes travel on the **Métro** and bus.

A "**Paris Visite**" ticket is valid for either 3 or 5 days and allows unlimited travel on the **Métro**, the whole bus network and the **RER** as well as the **Montmartre** Funicular.

- 1-3 Zones (excludes airports)

- 1-5 Zones (includes airports and Disney station)

There are also 1 day **Formule 1** tickets covering Zones 1-3. They may be bought at:

- Main Stations

- Paris airports

- Paris Tourist Office - **Champs Elysées**

Just the Ticket?

a second class return to ...	un aller et retour en seconde pour ...
a second class single to Paris please	un aller simple en seconde pour Paris svp
aisle seat	place côté couloir fs
are bikes carried free?	le transport des vélos est gratuit?
are there any weekend rates?	existe-t-il des forfaits de fin de semaine?
better value	plus intéressant
book of first class tickets (Métro)	carnet de première ms
book of second class tickets (Métro)	carnet de seconde ms
booking fee	prix de la réservation ms
booking obligatory	réservation obligatoire fs
Bus Station	Gare Routière
can motorbikes be carried?	on peut faire transporter les motos?
can one book in advance?	peut-on réserver à l'avance?
can one stopover?	c'est un billet avec faculté d'arrêt?
cancel	annuler
Carte Orange tickets	les coupons magnétiques de Carte Orange
categories 3 and 4 (see TGV timetables)	niveau 3 et 4
change one's reservation	modifier sa réservation
change the journey	modifier le voyage
cheapest fare	prix le plus avantageux ms
compulsory in both 1st and 2nd Class	obligatoire en première comme en seconde classe
connection by shuttle	correspondance par navette
connection	correspondance fs
departure station	gare de départ fs
departure	départ ms
destination	destination fs
do I have to validate the ticket?	faut-il composter le billet?

Do Not Open Doors	Ne Pas Ouvrir les Portes Soi-Même
Do Not Stand On Exit Steps	Il est Interdit de Stationner dans l'Emmarchement
Do not use folding seats in Rush Hour	En Cas d'Affluence, Ne Pas Utiliser les Strapontins
do you mind if I open the window?	ça ne vous fait rien si je baisse la glace?
does it cost more?	y a-t-il un supplément?
does one buy them at the tobacconists?	on les achète au bureaux de tabac?
does one have to book in advance?	doit-on réserver à l'avance?
does one have to change platform?	faut-il changer de quai?
does one have to change stations?	faut-il changer de gare?
double decker train	train à étage ms
Emergency Exit	Sortie de Secours
every half hour	toutes les demie-heures
Exit Without Ticket	Pour Sortir, Avancez sans Mettre votre Billet
fare stage	section fs
fare to ...	prix du billet pour ... ms.
folding seat on bus / train	strapontin ms
folding seat	siège à assise relevable ms
for a same day departure	pour un départ le jour même
for a week	pour une semaine
for London?	pour Londres?
for the weekend	pour le week-end
for three days	pour trois jours
from platform 19	du quai numéro dix-neuf
full fare	plein tarif
get out at ...	descendez à ...
go down / descend	descendez
guaranteed connections	des horaires synchronisés mpl
have you any special rates?	proposez-vous des tarifs spéciaux?
how far are we from ... ?	à quelle distance sommes-nous de ... ?
how many stops are there between here and ... ?	combien d'arrêts y a-t-il d'ici à ... ?
I wish to change my day of travel	je souhaite modifier le jour de mon voyage
I'd like a seat ...	je voudrais une place ...
in 1st class	en 1ère classe
In Emergency Smash Glass	En Cas d'Urgence Briser la Fenêtre
In Emergency, Turn Handles and Push	En Cas de Danger-Tournez les poignées et pousser
In Rush Hour	Aux Heures d'Affluence / de Pointe
in second class	en 2ème classe
in the front / rear / middle	à l'avant / à l'arrière / au milieu
is it cheaper off-peak?	ça coûte moins cher en période bleue?
is it far from here?	est-ce loin d'ici?
is there a cheap rate?	y a-t-il un tarif réduit?
is there a No Smoking compartment?	y a-t-il un compartiment non-fumeurs?

is there a restaurant car?	y a-t-il un wagon-restaurant?
is this seat taken / free?	cette place est-elle occupée / libre?
is this ticket valid for ... ?	ce billet est-il valable pour ... ?
last minute booking	réservation de dernière minute
left luggage ticket	bulletin de consigne ms
Limit of Validity of Tickets	Limite de la Validité des Billets
luggage locker	consigne automatique fs
Main Lines	Grandes Lignes
main station	grande gare fs
make a booking	effectuer une réservation
Meeting Point	Point Rencontre
Métro system	réseau RATP ms
Métro Train	Rame fs
not Saturdays and Sundays	sauf samedis et dimanches
offers a daily service	offre un service quotidien
off-peak (rail)	période bleue fs
on TGV's	dans les TGV
on the hour and the half hour	à l'heure et à la demie
on the spot fine	amende avec paiement immédiat fs
onboard catering	restauration à bord fs
open dated return	billet sans réservation de retour ms
optional	facultatif (-ve)
passengers from ...	voyageurs en provenance de ...
Passengers Only	Accès Strictement Réservé aux Passagers
peak period	période rouge fs
platform ticket	ticket d'accès au quai
Pull the Doors	Tirer sur les Portes
rail / road / bus ...	... ferroviaire / des transports routiers / des bus
Rear (Front) of Train for Dourdan	Dourdan - en queue (tête)
reduced price	PR (Prix Réduit)
refundable	remboursable
restaurant service	restauration fs
return (for ticket)	aller-retour ms
route map	plan du réseau ms
season ticket	carte jaune / orange fs
seat if available	place selon disponibilité fs
seat reservation	réservation en place assise fs
single (ticket)	aller simple ms
Special Fare / Special Fare applies	Tarification Spéciale
special rate	forfait ms / formules spéciales fpl
standby ticket	billet sans garantie ms
Suburban Lines (inc. RER)	Trains de Banlieue

take a ticket at the machine	prenez un ticket au distributeur
take this line from ... to ... station	prenez cette ligne en direction de ... jusqu'à la Gare ...
TGV supplement	supplément en TGV ms
TGV's serving Paris	TGV desservant Paris mpl
the ... train leaves from which platform / at what time?	le train pour ... part de quel quai / à quelle heure?
the amount refunded varies according to …	le montant remboursé varie selon …
the category of TGV	le niveau du TGV 1, 2, 3 ou 4
the class of TGV in which you travel	niveau de TGV emprunté ms
the connection with the RER B	la connexion avec le RER B
the price of the ticket varies according to ...	le prix du billet varie selon ...
the Railway Station / Bus Station	Gare SNCF / Gare Routière fs
the TGV guide	le guide pour le TGV
there is a delay?	y a-t-il un retard?
there is a mistake on my ticket	il y a une erreur sur mon billet
there is a train / bus how often?	il y a un train / bus tous les combien?
ticket collector	contrôleur ms
Ticket Office	Billetterie
ticket validation machine	machine à composter les billets fs
timetable	tableau horaire ms
To Platforms	Accès aux quais / voies
Train Departure Boards	Tableaux des trains au Départ

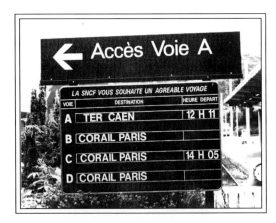

Train Departures	Trains au Départ
travel ticket	titre de transport ms
travelator / moving walkway	Trottoir Roulant
travelling 1st Class	voyager en première classe
Trolley Point	Point Chariots
unlimited Métro travel	un nombre illimité de voyages dans le Métro

vacant seat	place inoccupée fs
what platform does the ... train leave from?	de quel quai part le train pour ... ?
what's the fare to ... ?	quel est le tarif pour ... ?
when does one check-in?	quand faut-il se présenter pour l'embarquement?
when is the rush hour?	quelles sont les heures de pointe?
where does one buy tickets?	où achète-on les billets?
where is the bus station?	où est la gare routière?
where is the left luggage?	où est la consigne?
will there be room?	y aura-t-il de la place?
will you tell me when we get there?	vous me le direz quand on arrivera?
window seat	place fs côté fenêtre / hublot
you get off after five stops	vous descendez au cinquième arrêt
You must validate Carte Orange and tickets	Carte Orange + Billets - Il faut nous valider c'est obligatoire

Hotel chains

For overnight stops: Hotels such as Formule 1 are very reasonably priced and allow booking-in by simply inserting a credit card at the door at any hour of the day or night. Prices are per room - often sleeping 3 or 4 people. If staying for more than one night you need to reconfirm each morning.

Small town hotels are often even better value

3

On the road

Traffic Signs

Absence de Feux - Priorité Bus	Bus Right of Way in Absence of Traffic Lights
Absence de Marquage	No White Lines
Absence d'éclairage	Unlit Section
Accès Chantier	Site Entrance
Accotements Meubles / Dénivelés	Unstable / Sloping Verges
Accotements Non Stabilisés	Soft Verge
Accotements Surbaissés	Low Verges
Affaissements	Subsidence
Aire de Repos	Rest Area
Allumez Vos Codes	Dipped Headlamps
Allumez Vos Feux / Phares	Switch on Headlights
Arrêt Autorisé pour Liaisons	Permitted Picking Up Area
Arrêt de Cars	Coach Stop
Arrêts Fréquents	Frequent Stops
Arrosage	Crop Watering
Attention - Feux Décalés	Care - Staggered Signals
Attention Ecole	Caution, School
Attention Travaux	Road Works Ahead
Autocar Arrêt	Bus Stop
Avancez Jusqu'aux Feux	Move Right Up to Lights
Axe Rouge	Red Route (No Stopping)
Bande d'Arrêt d'Urgence Neutralisée sur 220m	No Hard Shoulder for 220m
Bandes de Ralentissement	Traffic Calming Strips
Bandes Axiales Effacées	No White Lines
Bandes Rugueuses	Rumble strips
Bandes Transversales	Sleeping Policemen
Bouchon	Traffic Holdup
Boue	Mud On Road
Bretelle	Motorway Link

Brouillard Fréquent	Frequent Fog
Brouillard - Soyez Prudents	Care - Fog
Carrefour Dangereux	Dangerous Crossroads
Carrefour Modifié	Changed Roundabout Layout
Carrefour Nouvellement Aménagé	New Roundabout Layout
Carrière	Quarry Exit

Cédez le Passage	Give Way
Centre - Bourg	Village Centre
Chantier d'Autoroute - Soyez Prudents	Motorway Works - Care
Chantier Interdit au Public	No Entry to Site
Chantier Mobile	Mobile Works Ahead
Chaussée Déformée	Poor Road Surface
Chutes de Pierres	Falling Rocks
Circulation Alternée	Traffic Control Ahead
Circulation Difficile	Slow Traffic
Circulation Interdite sur Bande d'Arrêt d'Urgence	Do Not Drive on Hard Shoulder
Circulez au Pas	Drive at Walking Pace
Contournement d'Uzerche	Uzerche Bypass
Contrôles Radar Fréquents	Frequent Radar Speed Checks
Convoi Exceptionnel	Wide / Slow Load
Côté de Stationnement	Parking This Side
Côté de Stationnement Permanent	Permanent Parking This Side
Côté du Stationnement Autorisé	Parking Allowed
Créneau de Dépassement dans X Km	Overtaking lane in X Km
Danger Eboulements	Risk Of Landslides
Danger en Rives	Dangerous Verges
Dénivellements d'Accotements	Sloping Verges
Descente Dangereuse	Dangerous Hill
Déviation	Detour, deviation
Emplacement à Louer	Space to Rent
Empruntez le Passage Souterrain	Use Underpass
Entrée Réglementée	Entry Restricted
Eteignez Vos Feux	Switch off Headlights
Fauchage	Hedge Trimming
Feux à 100m	Traffic Lights in 100m

Fin d'Allumage des Feux	Turn off Headlamps
Fin de Déviation	End of Deviation
Fin de Section Aménagée	End of Road Improvements
Fin de Zone de Stationnement Réglementé	End of Restricted Parking
Fin d'Interdiction de Dépasser	End of No Overtaking Zone
Fin Provisoire d'Autoroute	Temporary End of Motorway
Flashes Allumés = Danger	Flashing Lights = Danger
Forte Déclivité	Steep Hill
Gardez Votre File	Stay in Lane
Gare Routière	Bus Station
Gravillons	Loose Chippings
Halte Péage	Stop - Toll
Hauteur Limitée à 4m	Height Limit 4m
Hauteur Limitée	Height Restriction
Hors Gabarit	Oversize Vehicles
Interdiction de Doubler	No Overtaking
Interdit Côté Droit / Gauche	No Parking on Right / Left
Interdit de ce côté	No Parking This Side
Interdit des Deux Côtés	No Parking on Either Side
Interdit du 16 à la fin du mois	No Parking from 16th to end of month
Interdit du 1er au 15 du mois	No Parking 1st-15th of month
Interdit Plus d'une Heure	No Parking for More Than 1 Hour
Interdit sauf aux Livraisons	Parking for Deliveries Only
Interdit sur Trottoir	No Parking on Pavement
Itinéraire Conseillé	Recommended Route
Itinéraire Modifié Obligatoire	Route Change
Itinéraire sans Carburants sur 20 Km	No Fuel for 20Km
Marquage au Sol Effacée	No Road Markings
Modification Récente des Lieux	New Road Layout
Nids de Poule	Potholes
Nouveau Carrefour Giratoire	New Roundabout Ahead
Nouveaux Tracés en Service	New Road Layout

Parking Réservé GIG - GIC	Parking for disabled ex-soldiers and civilians

Par Temps de Pluie	(Road Slippery) In Rainy Weather
Passage à Niveau	Level Crossing
Passage Interdit	No Entry
Passage Métallique	Cattle Grid
Passage Protégé	Priority
Passages Successifs	Multiple Pedestrian Crossings
Péage	Toll
Peinture	Road Marking In Progress
Périphérique	Ring Road
Petite Ceinture	Inner Ring Road
Piétons - Traversez en Deux Temps	Pedestrians - Cross to the middle
Piétons	Pedestrians
Piste Réservée aux Transports Publics	Bus Lane
Poids Lourds	HGV's
Pont Etroit	Narrow Bridge
Pour Rennes Suivre Paris	For Rennes Follow Paris Signs
Prenez le Ticket	Take Ticket
Préparez votre Monnaie	Have Exact Money Ready
Prévention Routière	Road Safety Organisation
Priorité Piétons	Pedestrians Have Priority
Prochaine Sortie 1Km	Next Exit 1Km
Rainurage	Grooved Surface
Ralentir - Travaux	Roadworks - Slow
Ralentir	Slow
Ralentisseurs	Speed Bumps
Ralentissez	Slow
Rappel	Reminder / Warning
Refuge 200m	Emergency Layby 200m
Refuge à 100m	Refuge at 100m
Remblais Récents	New (i.e. unstable / soft) Verges
Réservé aux Piétons	Pedestrians Only
Risque de Bouchon	Tailback Likely
Risque de Brouillard	Risk of Fog
Risque de Projections d'eau	Spray From Surface Water
Risque d'Inondations par Temps de Pluie	Flood Risk
Rive Gauche / Droite	Left / Right Bank
Roulez Au Pas	Drive At Walking Speed
Route Barrée à 100m	Road Blocked in 100m
Sable	Sand On Road
Sauf Ayants Droit	Authorized Traffic Only
Sauf Caravanes	Except caravans
Sauf Desserte Locale	Except Local Deliveries
Sauf Pour Liaisons	Picking Up and Setting Down Only
Sauf Riverains	Residents Only
Sauf sur Trottoir	Except on Pavement
Sauf Transports en Commun	Except Public Transport

Section Péage sur 10 Km	10Km Toll Section
Sentier Pédestre	Footpath
Serrez à Droite	Keep Right
Signal Automatique	Automatic Signal
Signalisation Provisoirement Hors Service	No Signals During Works
Sortie Acquigny 200m	Turn Off to Acquigny 200m
Sortie de Camions	Lorry Exit
Sortie de Chantier	Site Exit
Sortie de Véhicules	Vehicle Exit
Sortie d'Engins	Beware Site Traffic
Sous Peine de Mise en Fourrière	Towaway Zone
Stat. Alterné Semi-Mensuel	Fortnightly Parking on alternate sides
Stationnement Autorisé au Trottoir	Parking Allowed on Pavement
Stationnement Autorisé	Parking Allowed
Stationnement Interdit	No Parking
Stationnement Réglementé	Parking Restricted
Stationnement Toléré Voitures de Tourisme	Private car Parking Allowed
Strictement Réservé aux Véhicules Habilités	Authorized Vehicles Only
Sur Toute la Longueur de la Voie	Along the Whole Carriageway
Testez vos Freins	Test Your Brakes
Tir de Mines	Blasting
Tous Véhicules	All Vehicles
Travaux Agricoles	Agricultural Work
Travaux en Cours	Road Works
Travaux sur 2 Km	Roadworks for 2 Km
Travaux sur RN 173	Roadworks on RN 173
Traversée d'Engins	Contractors' Traffic Crossing
Traversée de (Saumur) Difficile	Holdups through (Saumur)
Tunnel Sous La Manche	Channel Tunnel
Utilisez Votre Frein Moteur	Use Low Gear
Véhicules Lents	Slow Vehicles
Véhicules Surbaissés - Attention	Low Vehicles - Risk of Grounding
Verglas Fréquent	Black Ice Frequent
Verglas	Icy Road
Virages	Bends
Voies Rétrécies	Narrow Lanes
Voie Express ms	Express Way
Voie Sans Issue	No Thoroughfare
Voie Semi-Piétonne	Semi-Pedestrianised Road
Voie Submersible	Road Liable to Flood
Voie Unique	Single Carriageway / Single Track
Vous n'avez pas la priorité	Give way
Zone d'Evitement	Escape Road

Planning the Journey by Road

The well-known yellow Michelin™ road maps are available for all regions of France. North / South reversible (red) versions are for longer journeys.

- **Michelin Regional Maps of France**

989	(1:1,000,000)	France

230	(1:200,000)	Brittany
231		Normandy
232		Pays de Loire
233		Poitou-Charentes
234		Aquitaine
235		Midi-Pyrénées
236		Nord: Flandres - Artois - Picardie
237		Paris Region
238		Centre
239		Auvergne - Limousin
240		Languedoc - Roussillon
241		Champagne - Ardennes
242		Alsace et Lorraine
243		Bourgogne - Franche-Comté
244		Rhône - Alpes
245		Provence - Côte d'Azur
246		Vallée du Rhône
276		Picardie

- **Detailed Maps - France**

51	(1:200,000)	Calais - Lille - Bruxelles
52		Le Havre - Dieppe - Amiens
53		Arras - Charleville - Mézières - St.Quentin
54		Cherbourg - Caen - Rouen
55		Caen - Rouen - Paris
56		Paris - Reims - Chalon-sur-Marne
57		Verdun - Metz - Wissembourg
58		Brest - Quimper - St.Brieuc
59		St. Brieuc - St.Malo - Rennes
60		Le Mans - Chartres - Paris
61		Paris - Troyes - Chaumont
62		Epinal - Nancy - Strasbourg
63		Vannes - La Baule - Angers
64		Angers - Tours - Orléans
65		Montargis - Auxerre - Dijon

66		Dijon - Besançon - Mulhouse
67		Nantes - Les Sables d'Olonne - Poitiers
68		Niort - Poitiers - Châteauroux
69		Bourges - Nevers - Macon
70		Beaune - Macon - Evian
71		La Rochelle - Royan - Bordeaux
72		Angoulême - Limoges - Guéret
73		Clermont-Ferrand - Vichy - Lyon
74		Lyon - Chambéry - Geneva
75		Bordeaux - Périgueux - Tulle
76		Aurillac - Le Puy - St.Etienne
77		Valence - Grenoble - Gap
78		Bordeaux - Dax - Biarritz
79		Bordeaux - Agen - Montauban
80		Albi - Rodez - Nîmes
81		Montélimar - Avignon - Digne
82		Mont-de-Marsan - Pau - Toulouse
83		Carcassonne - Montpellier - Nîmes
84		Marseille - Toulon - Nice
85		Biarritz - Lourdes - Luchon
86		Luchon - Andorra - Perpignan
87		Vosges - Alsace
88		Clermont-Ferrand - Lyon - St. Etienne
89		Evian - Annecy - Briançon
90		Corsica
101	(1:53,000)	Outskirts of Paris
106	(1:100,000)	Environs of Paris
110	(1:60,000)	Lyon and environs
111	(1:50,000)	Grand Lille
114	(1:100,000)	French Riviera - Var - Verdon Gorges
115		French Riviera - Maritime Alps
1031		Environs of Toulouse
1033		Environs of Bordeaux
1044		Environs of Nantes
1063		Environs of Clermont-Ferrand

- **Other Publications - France**

Main Road Maps

989	(1:1,000,000)	France
910	(1:2,200,000)	France administrative
911	(1:1,000,000)	France route planning
914		France motorways atlas
915		France main roads atlas
916		France (reversible)

918		France - north
919		France - south

Atlases

92	(1:200,000)	Motoring atlas France - spiral bound
96		Motoring atlas France - paperback
97		Motoring atlas France - hardback

Bleu and / or Town and City Plans

(published by Grafocarte)

Bordeaux	Caen
Cannes	Clermont-Ferrand
Dijon	Le Havre
Lille	Lourdes
Marseille	Monaco
Nice	Rouen
St Malo	Toulouse

City Plans - Paris - Michelin

7	(1:20,000)	Paris tourism
9		Paris transport
10	(1:10,000)	Paris plan
11		Paris atlas
12		Paris plan (street index)
18	(1:15,000)	North west suburbs (street index)
20		North east suburbs (street index)
22		South west suburbs (street index)
24		South east suburbs (street index)
25		Atlas Paris and suburbs
101	(1:53,000)	Outskirts of Paris
106	(1:100,000)	Environs of Paris
237	(1:200,000)	Paris region

Disneyland, Paris Plan Guide
Disneyland, Paris Green Guide

Green Tourist Guides

These guides cover most areas of France although not all are available in English.

Specialist Maps

Michelin also produce a series of historical maps.

The Regions and Departments of France

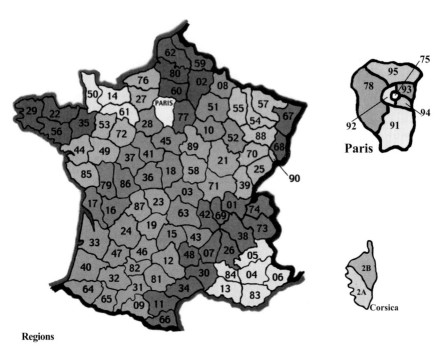

Paris

Corsica

Regions

Alsace	67, 68
Aquitaine	24, 33, 40, 47, 64
Auvergne	03, 15, 43, 63
Basse-Normandie	14, 61, 50
Bourgogne	21, 58, 71, 89
Bretagne (Brittany)	22, 29, 35, 56
Centre	18, 28, 36, 37, 41, 45
Champagne-Ardenne	08, 10, 51, 52
Corse (Corsica)	2A, 2B
Franche-Comté	25, 39, 70, 90
Haute-Normandie	27, 76
Ile-de-France	75, 77, 78, 91, 92, 93, 94, 95
Languedoc Roussillon	11, 30, 34, 48, 66
Limousin	19, 23, 87
Lorraine	54, 55, 57, 88
Midi-Pyrénées	09, 12, 31, 32, 46, 65, 81, 82
Nord Pas de Calais	59, 62
Pays de la Loire	44, 49, 53, 72, 85
Picardie	02, 60, 80
Poitou-Charentes	16, 17, 79, 86
Provence-Alpes Côte d'Azur	04, 05, 06, 13, 83, 84
Rhône-Alpes	01, 07, 26, 38, 42, 69, 73, 74

Départements

01	Ain	48	Lozère
02	Aisne	49	Maine et Loire
03	Allier	50	Manche
04	Alpes de Haute Provence	51	Marne
05	Hautes Alpes	52	Haute Marne
06	Alpes Maritimes	53	Mayenne
07	Ardèche	54	Meurthe et Moselle
08	Ardennes	55	Meuse
09	Ariège	56	Morbihan
10	Aube	57	Moselle
11	Aude	58	Nièvre
12	Aveyron	59	Nord
13	Bouches du Rhône	60	Oise
14	Calvados	61	Orne
15	Cantal	62	Pas de Calais
16	Charente	63	Puy de Dôme
17	Charente Maritime	64	Pyrénées Atlantiques
18	Cher	65	Hautes Pyrénées
19	Corrèze	66	Pyrénées Orientales
2A	Corse du Sud	67	Bas Rhin
2B	Haute Corse	68	Haut Rhin
21	Côte d'Or	69	Rhône
22	Côtes du Nord	70	Haute-Saône
23	Creuse	71	Saône-et Loire
24	Dordogne	72	Sarthe
25	Doubs	73	Savoie
26	Drôme	74	Haute Savoie
27	Eure	75	Paris
28	Eure et Loir	76	Seine Maritime
29	Finistère	77	Seine et Marne
30	Gard	78	Yvelines
31	Haute-Garonne	79	Deux Sèvres
32	Gers	80	Somme
33	Gironde	81	Tarn
34	Hérault	82	Tarn et Garonne
35	Ille et-Vilaine	83	Var
36	Indre	84	Vaucluse
37	Indre et Loire	85	Vendée
38	Isère	86	Vienne
39	Jura	87	Haute Vienne
40	Landes	88	Vosges
41	Loir et Cher	89	Yonne
42	Loire	90	Territoire de Belfort
43	Haute Loire	91	Essonne
44	Loire Atlantique	92	Hauts-de-Seine
45	Loiret	93	Seine St Denis
46	Lot	94	Val de Marne
47	Lot et Garonne		

Useful tips

- The international road sign system, with some additions, operates in France. Traffic is on the righthand side of the road and it is important to remember to look left when emerging from a stationary position and to keep to the right!

- If you have a passenger, agree on a safe procedure for overtaking. It is maybe wise to avoid the use of "No" and "Go" because they can be misheard. Use perhaps "Wait" and "OK".

- Road Classification
  Autoroutes - Motorways - shown yellow with red border   e.g. A 10
  Route Nationale - Main roads - marked in red   e.g. N 113 or RN 113
  Route Départementale - Secondary Roads - shown in Yellow   e.g. D 122 or RD 122
  Route Communale - local roads - marked in white   e.g. C 650 or CD 650
  Dangerous Roads e.g. narrow mountain roads with bad surfaces are striped yellow and red

- D Roads are often an excellent alternative to the Routes Nationales as they are frequently of a very high standard and far less busy. They are sometimes marked on maps in red if they are more important! One small disadvantage is that laybys are less common or non-existent and petrol stations rare.

- Maps are often very unreliable once you get off the beaten track. Roads may be marked which do not exist or may exist but are not shown. D roads may also be wrongly numbered.

- **Bornes kilométriques**, the continental version of milestones, are marked with the road number as well as the distance to the next town. They have either red or yellow tops according to the class of road.

- Danger! Traffic emerging from the right, even from minor streets, still has priority in many urban areas. If in doubt, GIVE WAY! Although **Priorité à Droite** is being phased out, you can **still** never be quite sure. At each junction the road to your right must be treated as having potential priority until the stop line or sign can be seen, even if you are on the main street! There is no logic or consistency whatsoever in the use of Stop / Give Way signs. Fortunately the day has now officially passed when farm vehicles could emerge from little lanes onto fast roads with complete impunity. Perhaps this generation has died out or been killed off by insisting on priority!

- There is no amber light before the green as in Britain.

- At night, traffic lights are sometimes switched to flashing amber for traffic approaching from all directions. This means proceed with caution!

- Traffic lights at roadworks do not use green, only flashing amber. It is very common for them to be ignored by motorists.

- Motorway and main road exits are well marked with luminescent green and white bollards.

- Motorways have emergency laybys - **Refuges** - on the hard shoulder - much safer than in the UK, since the risk of a rear shunt is less and the emergency lane is kept free for emergency vehicles.

- The line marking off the motorway Hard Shoulder consists of long dashes. You are intended to check the distance between your vehicle and the one in front as you are driving alongside this line by using the dashes as a measure: 1 Dash between vehicles = Danger   2 Dashes = Safety

- The police often check motorway tickets and because they are time-stamped can see how fast you have been travelling …!

- France now has what is arguably the best road system in Europe but the accident and death rates are still twice as bad as in the UK. Many drivers do not realize the dangers of tailgating - a distance of a couple of metres behind is very common - and will overtake on blind mountain bends as well as cutting across traffic from the outside lane to take an exit slip road on motorways.

- Pedestrian crossings are largely ignored by all except foreign drivers. They are however an apparent source of pride to the local community, which trumpets the existence of these **Passages Successifs** at the entrance to a village along with the **Commerces, Eglise du XIV siècle** etc. They are of different colours, eg green or red as well as the more prosaic black and white stripes. Some are raised as well as coloured.

- At some junctions, there is a light with a green cross in the centre to warn of traffic coming from opposite.

- Similar red crosses tell you to assume that opposing traffic is halted.

- There are no traffic lights on the opposite side of the junction, so it is important to stop where you can see the small, angled "repeater" lights low down on the post.

- Pay particular attention to main traffic lights, as these are sometimes not working and generally very dimly lit. Flashing amber means you can proceed with caution - often to the right, where there is usually a crossing around the corner. This is a signal for motorists to attempt to run over the unfortunate pedestrian trying to cross the road while the lights are in the walker's favour. The trick is to keep walking since the motorist will then (probably) miss you!

- Road signing other than on motorways can be haphazard; the signs non-existent or hidden, often behind trees or visible only from another direction at junctions. Signs are frequently angled so that either conclusion may be drawn - straight ahead or right. Some signs are put on walls of buildings in towns at a previous junction so that the unwary motorist finds himself turning into a side road or a supermarket prior to the intended route.

- Traffic already on roundabouts has priority but many motorists will ignore this rule, perhaps because, illogically, it runs counter to the notorious "**priorité à droite**" rule. A new pamphlet has been issued, some sixteen years after the changes in the traffic rules on roundabouts, to try yet again to educate French motorists on the necessity for correct procedure.

- Some roundabouts are totally different from the norm in that **traffic already on them must give way to vehicles entering from the right! There are even roundabouts with 4 give ways, each at 90 degrees, but they are unusual!**

- The French motorways are privately run and tolls are levied on all the **autoroutes à péage** . There are some free stretches however, especially around certain towns such as Clermont Ferrand. The sign is a white car on a rectangular blue background.

- Signs to **Autoroutes** often give the impression that there will be no choice of turnoffs for other main roads before you reach the motorway. Sometimes it is a calculated gamble.

- Motorway service stations with full facilities are every 40 km and there are also **aires de repos** or rest areas. Overnight areas are provided for caravans and motorcaravans.

- Some toll barriers are automatic and exact change is required - keep coins ready. Visa (**Carte Bleue** in France) and Mastercard are accepted.

- In the event of a breakdown or an accident on a motorway, the police must be contacted by using the emergency telephones situated every 2 km on orange posts. They will then send out a garage. Only a **dépanneur agréé** (Authorized Breakdown Mechanic) is allowed. He will arrive within 30 minutes, repair your car on the spot or tow you to the nearest garage. Basic tariffs and extra charges are displayed on the emergency telephones and also on the breakdown vehicles. Between 6pm and 8am and on Saturdays, Sundays and public holidays the rates go up by 25%.

- On motorways the orange phone boxes have lights which flash to warn of hazard ahead.

- In the event of total electrical failure, put the hazard warning triangle 30 m behind your vehicle where it must be visible for 100 metres to vehicles approaching in the same lane. Hazard flashers should also be lit as an extra precaution if they are still functional.

- Navigation can be a real problem since Spain may be signposted but not the next town!

- Many towns are signposted only from the centre out so that the driver passing through will be unable to see the signs since they will be blank on his side of the junction.

- Some junctions are signposted for traffic coming from one direction only, even on main roads away from towns. The motorist has therefore to stop and look back.

- On roundabouts, prior warning of exits is not always given and last minute decisions have to be made when actually on the roundabout.

- Some streets in towns are semi-pedestrianised, so great care is needed on the part of both drivers and those on foot. Regulations for traffic are found at the entrance to the street or area.

- Road markings are often effaced and are difficult to see.

- On the approach to junctions, be aware that the right hand lane may signal straight ahead but at the last moment will, as if by magic, allow only a right turn. This is especially important as the average motorist will not allow you to change lanes.

- It is quite common for traffic signs to show the direction to a particular town as being, for example, right at the next junction, only to inform the hapless motorist at the crossroads themselves that s/he should be in a totally different lane since the required destination is now straight ahead!

- Town and village boundary exits are shown by a diagonal red line through the name.

- Often there is only one sign to a particular place and no more. Perhaps the French motorist is blessed with second sight! Examples are places of interest such as viewpoints. Maybe it is done to encourage the art of conversation since stopping to ask the way is then essential!

- In the country, the entry to side roads is indicated by red and white posts which make it easy to see, especially at night.

- Cross roads signs are not a true representation of the layout. Thus an *X* may warn of a **T** junction ahead.

Legal requirements

- The minimum age for driving in France is 18. EU Nationals need a valid national driving licence only; nationals of non-EU countries an international driving licence. The registration papers (log book) must be carried and a GB plate of the approved size should be affixed to the rear of the vehicle. Up to date information can be obtained from motoring organizations.

- On steep gradients, the vehicle going downhill must give way. If one vehicle has to reverse, it is the one without a trailer which does so (or the lighter if neither is towing).

- Seat belts must be worn - front and rear.

- Helmets must be worn on mopeds and motorbikes.

- Headlights must be converted to dip to the right by using an adhesive strip or a conversion kit.

- Yellow headlights are no longer required.

- A spare set of bulbs is compulsory in France.

- A First Aid kit is advisable but not compulsory.

- Warning triangle or use of hazard flashers is compulsory. (30m behind - more if on a bend - must be visible for 100m to driver approaching in the same lane).

- Dipped headlights in daytime are compulsory for motorcycles larger than 125cc.

Care!

- Remember that flashing one's headlights is not taken to mean that you are allowing someone precedence - quite the opposite in fact: It means "look out I am coming through"! Lorry drivers, especially those who are widely travelled, are however aware of its international use and their potentially ambiguous signals are thus to be treated with suitable caution.

- Traffic violations, even relatively minor ones, are heavily punished. Pleading guilty to the police can avoid court action and even reduce the fine. Nevertheless, very large on the spot fines are still levied. A receipt should always be obtained. Payment must be made in French Francs. Credit cards are not accepted, although Travellers Cheques in French Francs may be. Refusal to pay a fine may entail immediate confiscation of the car. The principal offences where this is also applied are: hit and run, failing to stop on request, driving when under the influence of alcohol. If a motorist does not wish to plead guilty, a deposit must be paid and a request made for the case to be heard in court. From every point of view, drinking and driving should be avoided on the Continent.

- Blood Alcohol Limit: France 0.05%   GB: 0.08%

- Car and Mobile Telephones not conforming to GSM standards could be confiscated because they can interfere with Emergency Radio Bands.

Speed limits

* Normal roads / weather conditions **90kph** (55 mph)

* Towns **50kph** (30 mph) in all conditions or sometimes **70kph** (44 mph) on important through roads

* Dual carriageways with two lanes in each direction and toll-free motorways **110kph** (68 mph)

* Motorways **130kph** (81 mph)

* Paris ring roads **80kph** (50 mph)

These limits are lower in rain and other adverse weather conditions:

* Motorways: **110kph** (68mph)

* Urban motorways and dual carriageways: **100kph** (62mph)

* Other roads: **80kph** (50mph)

There is a minimum speed of **80kph** (50mph) in daylight on motorways for the left hand lane if visibility and conditions are good

---

A road sign with a white edged yellow square means that you have priority. The same square with a diagonal black line, as illustrated, means that **you do not have priority on that road** but the priority lies with those entering from the right.

Beware!

- Motorway service station pump attendants sometimes carry out fraudulent oil level checks. They reinsert the dipstick part way after wiping it. The oil level thus appears to be low and they then pretend to empty a can into the sump filler. Not only do they pocket the cost of the oil, but they will also solicit a tip!

- When parking and leaving a caravan or trailer, be sure to clamp it or leave someone on guard. Theft of caravans at supermarkets near Channel Ports is common and it only takes an expert a few moments!

- Beware the "helpful" person who drives alongside and flags you down to point out something wrong with your vehicle. It is often a preliminary to theft or worse. Drive on and check when at a safe distance and in a safe public place.

- Currency scams are also not unknown at frontier filling stations where foreign notes are accepted! It pays to check the exchange rate!! (or pay by credit card).

The road chaos at the beginning and end of August, when all of France seems to be on the move, is best avoided as are the days before and after **jours fériés** or Public Holidays and many weekends (Friday - Sunday midday). When a Bank Holiday occurs on a Thursday or a Tuesday, many organizations tend to **faire le pont** that is, bridge the gap with the weekend.

Alternative Routes or **itinéraires bis** (sometimes just **Bis** for short) are intended to take motorists away from the usually congested Holiday routes. Signs are green with yellow panels bearing the legend **BIS**. There are more than 90 roadside

Welcome and Information Centres which provide free maps and help to motorists. Some are open 24 hours.

A colourful cartoon character, **le Bison Futé** (Crafty Bison) -from **Itinéraire BIS** meaning alternative or holiday route - is used to publicise Holiday Route Information from the **Sécurité Routière** which issues a **Calendrier du Trafic Routier** widely available from tourist offices. This gives an annual forecast of traffic difficulties in a handy, easily-read form.

- Yellow signs with black lettering are used for diversions (**déviations**).

- Temporary road markings are yellow.

- Road Traffic Information Centres (**Centres d'Information Routière**) supply the latest data by telephone on current road conditions as well as forecasts of traffic congestion for some considerable time ahead.

Travel Information

Radio:

Autoroute 107.7 FM   An excellent source of information in French and English on all French motorway conditions

Telephone:

Allô Bonjour	Tel: 01 49 52 53 54
Autoroute Information:	Tel: 01 47 05 90 01

COFIROUTEL:
For Autoroutes A11 / A81
L'Océane, A10 L'Aquitaine   Tel: 01 36 68 10 77
and A71 Orléans Bourges

INFOTRAFIC A1:
(For the Autoroute du Nord)   Tel: 01 05 43 14 31
or
Centre National de Rosny   Tel: 02 48 94 33 33

Centres Régionaux:

Bordeaux:	Tel: 05 56 96 33 33
Ile de France:	Tel: 02 48 99 33 33
Lille:	Tel: 03 20 47 33 33
Lyon:	Tel: 04 78 54 33 33
Marseille:	Tel: 04 91 78 78 78
Metz:	Tel: 03 87 63 33 33
Rennes:	Tel: 02 99 32 33 33

Weather forecasts

For the **Département** of your choice: 08 36 68 02
+ number of Department (eg Manche 50).

For Metropolitan France: 08 36 68 01 01
Details of 24 hour filling stations are also obtainable
from the above but - a word of caution! These are
not always manned and are therefore card operated.
Most accept only **Cartes Bleues,** but this situation is likely to change.

Information is also available on Road Travel: **Minitel Bison Futé: 36 - 15 ROUTE.**

It never rains…

(temperatures) markedly above	des valeurs nettement supérieures
a few drops of rain here and there	quelques gouttes ci et là
a few showers are possible	quelques ondées possibles
be hot	faire très chaud
be warm	faire chaud
be nice (weather)	faire beau
be windy	faire du vent
becoming variable	devenant variable
calm sea	mer belle
dampness	humidité fs
flash of lightning	éclair ms
heavy showers	des averses orageuses
is it usually as hot / cold?	fait-il toujours aussi chaud / froid?
it is pouring	il pleut à verse
it is raining / snowing / thundering	il pleut / neige / tonne
it will be sunnier in the afternoon	le soleil se montrera davantage l'après-midi
it will feel a lot cooler tomorrow	demain, sensation de fraîcheur très marqué
light wind, south to south-east	vent faible de sud à sud-est
north / north-east / north west wind	vent de secteur nord / nord-est / nord-ouest
rainy weather	un temps pluvieux
the weather will remain unsettled	le temps restera agité
there are floods	il y a des inondations fpl
there is a north-west wind blowing	c'est un vent de nord-ouest qui souffle
there is going to be a storm	il va faire de l'orage
there will be bright periods	il y aura des éclaircies fpl
thunder	tonnerre ms
to blow	souffler

Fuel

Prices must be displayed at the entrance to the filling station and are also shown at motorway slip roads for the next five stations. Repeat notices are about 1/2 mile before the next rest area with petrol facilities. Fuel is very much cheaper at **"Grandes Surfaces"** (Hypermarkets). Petrol pump attendants on **Autoroutes** expect a tip!

For those towing caravans, access to pumps may be extremely narrow or otherwise difficult.

If you are not on a main road, bear in mind that you may have difficulty in getting fuel during the lunch break. Driving through towns is however much easier at this time.

Problems with the quality of 95 octane unleaded petrol have been reported for some time. It could be prudent to use Super 98 unleaded instead.

•	Super	4 star 97 octane
•	Sans plomb 95, Eurosuper 95 or SP 95 lead-free petrol	
•	Sans plomb 98	4 star lead-free petrol
•	Essence ordinaire	ordinary petrol
•	Gazole / Gasoil	Diesel fuel
•	GPL	LPG (Liquid Petroleum Gas)

Parking Regulations

- In Paris and most large towns there are restricted and paying parking zones (blue and grey zones); tickets must be obtained from the ticket machine (**horodateur** - small change is required) and displayed (inside the windscreen on the driver's side); failure to display may result in a heavy fine. Be careful where you leave your vehicle - Paris traffic wardens are not noted for their generosity and sweet nature, even towards tourists.

- Parking in many towns is permitted, even provided for, on pavements. Street parking is often restricted to alternate sides according to whether it is the first or second half of the month. (See the circular blue and red signposts). Sometimes parking is not allowed at all for half of the month (See also Road Signs and English-French vocabulary).

- A useful clue to market days is the early morning till perhaps mid-afternoon prohibition of parking on certain days.

- Blue painted lines and signs indicate a **Zone Bleue** requiring a parking disc which is obtainable from various outlets in the town; police stations, tourist offices and certain shops. Time of arrival must be indicated on the clock face. Length of stay is limited to one hour and a half between 0900 and 1900 (except between 1130 and 1430). Parking is not regulated on Public Holidays and Sundays.

Taxis

Passengers' rights:

- No taxi driver can refuse a fare if the taxi is free. "Free" is interpreted as follows:

    - When the taxi is stationary and its sign is not covered.

    - When the taxi is in motion, the sign is lit and the driver is not due to finish his shift in half an hour.

- No disabled passengers may be refused even when they need help. Such passengers' wheel chairs must be transported.

- The driver must take the shortest route but you may indicate which you prefer.

- Smoking is allowed if there is no sign to the contrary.

- The driver must not smoke unless there is a partition.

- At the end of the journey a receipt must be issued at the request of the passenger or when the journey costs more than 100F. This receipt must bear the registration number of the taxi.

- It is customary to tip the driver but the latter cannot demand it.

- The usual tip is 10-15%.

- The passenger decides whether the window should be opened or closed.

- You may set down or pick up someone you know during the journey. No extra charge must be made, but the driver has the right to turn the clock back to zero to show the minimum charge again for each stop.

A taxi driver has the right to refuse to transport you if:

- you are accompanied by more than two adults (two children under ten count as one adult).

- you want to sit next to him.

- you have too much luggage or it is too heavy to be carried.

- because of your dress or your luggage the interior of the vehicle may be damaged or made dirty.

- if you hail the driver when you are less than 50 metres from a taxi rank.

- The driver can refuse to wait for you where parking is limited, not allowed or impossible.

Taxi Meters

- The meter shows the cost of the journey either:

   according to the distance covered, if the speed of the taxi is greater than 37kph

   or:

   time elapsed if the speed is less.

- The window must be lit and the cost of the journey permanently visible to the passenger.

When you telephone for a taxi, the cost of the journey to pick you up is added to the cost of the subsequent distance covered.

Coach Travel

Long distance coaches are a rarity, apart from those run by Eurolines.

Paris Coach Stations:

Eurolines	3-5, Avenue de la Porte de la Villette
	Paris 19e Tel: 01 40 38 93 93
	Avenue de la Porte de Charenton
	Paris 12e Tel: 01 43 44 54 44

Car Rental

- There are agencies at airports, air terminals, railway stations and in main streets. There are also smaller local firms, to be found in **Les Pages Jaunes** (Yellow Pages).

- Automatic cars are available on demand but are less usual.

- You must show a valid UK driving licence, held for a minimum of a year, as well as a passport.

- The minimum age is 21, except in some cases where it is 23.

- Deposits are only necessary where credit cards are not used.

- In comparing costs, ask if insurance is included and what type.

- Third Party is compulsory whereas collision damage waiver and comprehensive are optional.

Insurance of hire vehicles:

- Rental firms each have their own conditions of hire, but most have similar arrangements to those quoted below. It cannot be emphasised strongly enough that the small print should be read and your liabilities (which may be considerable) understood before you sign the contract.

- All vehicles must be covered by a basic Third Party insurance which idemnifies against public liability i.e. injury to people other than the occupants of the vehicle and damage to property other than the vehicle.

- Most firms also offer insurance for damage to the vehicle in excess of a fixed sum but will often include fire and broken windscreen cover in the basic tariff.

- Theft is usually subject to an excess, which may or may not be purchasable.

- Breakdown costs, oil and customs documents are generally included in the basic hire charge. Recovery of the vehicle may **not** be at the cost of the Hire Firm.

- Not included and non-purchasable as a package are traffic fines and fuel.

- Hirers can usually "buy" the excess, i.e. insure against the cost of possible accidental damage to the vehicle by paying a fixed sum. Thus no excess charge would be levied in the case of accident. This is well worth considering. (But see below).

- Some (usually smaller) firms, in the case of commercial vehicles, **still** make collision damage to the upper part of the vehicle the responsibility of the hirer, **even when Collision Damage Waiver has been paid!! Read the small print - again!!**

- **Some, even the largest, "may" (they say), charge a flat-rate non-waivable excess in the event of theft. Some say that a charge "will" be made.**

- Insurance of the driver and passengers is usually an optional extra.

- Mileage charges, if in force, can greatly increase cost if long trips are contemplated.

Some commonly used terms in Vehicle Hire Contracts:

European subsidiaries of the giant American Rental Agencies often use American / English abbreviations even in their French language brochures:

CDW	Collision Damage Waiver (usually) avoids "excess"
TPC	Theft Protection Coverage (usually) avoids "excess"
PAI	Personal Accident Insurance

Rachat de Franchise en cas de collision	CDW
Assurance suppression franchise	CDW
Assurance conducteur-passagers	Driver / passenger insurance

- Again, beware the CDW clause which requires the **identification** of a Third Party as being involved in the damage! Car Park damage in your absence would not be covered - unless of course the person kindly leaves you a note admitting his liability!

- Personal Accident and Theft Insurance cover will inevitably contain exclusions, notably on extent and amount of cover and will probably require guarded parking between specified hours.

Car Hire at Railway Stations

Avis + Train in 200 French towns. Preferential rates for rail travellers. Bookable in advance at stations and travel agents. Information from Avis on : (Paris) 01 46 10 60 60

Cycle Hire

Bicycles are for hire at many railway stations as well as from specialist shops. Look for the sign **"Location de VTT"** (for mountain bikes), or **"Location de vélos"** (for tourers).

Hire It Here!

(fairly) powerful car	une voiture (assez) nerveuse
a small / big / medium-sized car	une petite / grande voiture / une voiture moyenne
according to your departure point	selon votre point de départ

advance booking is compulsory	la réservation est obligatoire
an automatic	une voiture automatique
are there any weekend rates?	existe-t-il des forfaits de fin de semaine?
availability	disponibilité fs
basic rate	tarif de base ms
before you leave	avant votre départ
better value	plus intéressant
booking centres	centrales de réservation fpl
booking fee included	réservation incluse / comprise
booking fee	prix de la réservation ms
booking obligatory	réservation obligatoire fs
booking	réservation fs
box (on a form)	case fs
bring back the car / bike	ramener la voiture / le vélo
can I pay by credit card?	puis-je payer par carte de crédit?
can I return the car in (town)?	puis-je ramener la voiture à (Ville)?
can you show me how the ... works?	pourriez-vous me montrer comment fonctionne ... ?
Car Hire Firms	Loueurs de Véhicules
change one's reservation	modifier sa réservation
collision waiver	rachat de franchise ms
comfortable	confortable
damage to property	dégâts matériels mpl
do I have to pay a deposit?	dois-je donner une caution?
does it cost more?	y a-t-il un supplément?
does one have to book in advance?	doit-on réserver à l'avance?
does that include mileage?	est-ce que cela comprend le kilométrage?
driving licence	permis de conduire ms
duration of your journey	la durée de votre itinéraire
for a week	pour une semaine
for another date	pour une autre date
for the weekend	pour le week-end
for three days	pour trois jours
glove box	boite à gants fs
go ahead with booking	procéder à la réservation
have it to hand	ayez-le à portée de la main
have you any special rates?	proposez-vous des tarifs spéciaux?
heading (on a form)	rubrique fs
here are my name and address	je vous donne mon nom et mon adresse
here is my driving licence	voici mon permis de conduire
hire agency	agence de location fs
hire contract	contrat de location ms

how many litres to 100km does it do?	elle fait combien au 100km?
how much is insurance?	combien coûte l'assurance?
how much is it to hire for an hour / day / week?	combien coûte la location à l'heure / à la journée / à la semaine?
how much is the deposit / fine?	quel est le montant de la caution / de la contravention?
how much is the deposit?	la caution s'élève à combien?
I prefer a small car	je préfère une petite voiture
I want fully comprehensive insurance	je voudrais une assurance tous risques
I want to report an accident	je voudrais signaler un accident
I would like to hire a car with driver	je voudrais louer une voiture avec chauffeur
I'd like to book ...	je voudrais réserver ...
I'd like to bring it back here	je voudrais la ramener ici
I'd like to hire a car / a bike	je voudrais louer une voiture / un vélo
I'd like to pick up the car here and return it at ...	je voudrais prendre la voiture ici et la rendre à ...
insurance documents	documents d'assurance
insurance policy	contrat d'assurance ms
is insurance included?	l'assurance est comprise?
is mileage included?	le kilométrage, est-il compris?
is there a cheap rate?	y a-t-il un tarif réduit?
is there a hire agency near here?	y a-t-il une agence de location près d'ici?
it is a hire car	c'est une voiture de location
it is a Renault / Rover / Citroën	c'est une Renault / Rover / Citroën
it is insured by the hire company	elle est assurée par la société de location
make a booking	effectuer une réservation
method of payment	moyen de paiement ms
my driving licence	mon permis de conduire
my home address is in ... (country)	je suis domicilié(e) en ... (pays)
no excess (insurance)	suppression de la franchise fs
on the back of the contract	au verso du contrat
passenger insurance	assurance-passagers fs
payment method	moyens de paiement mpl
please fill in this form	voulez-vous bien remplir ce formulaire
reduced price	PR (Prix Réduit)
refundable	remboursable
so as to avoid possible extra charges	afin d'éviter d'éventuels frais supplémentaires
special rate	forfait ms / formules spéciales fpl

Asking the Way

above ...	au dessus de ...
am I on the right road for ... ?	suis-je sur la bonne route pour ... ?

at the crossroads	au carrefour
at the pedestrian crossing	au passage cloûté
at the roundabout	au rond-point / au sens giratoire
behind	derrière
can you recommend ... ?	pouvez-vous recommander ... ?
can you tell me how to find ... ?	pouvez-vous me dire comment trouver... ?
can you tell me how to get to ... ?	pouvez-vous me dire comment aller ... ?
can you tell me the best way to Paris?	pouvez-vous m'indiquer le meilleur chemin pour Paris?
can you tell me the way to ... ?	pourriez-vous m'indiquer le chemin pour aller à ... ?
carry straight on	vous continuez
cross	traversez
don't mention it	je vous en prie
excuse me ... , I have lost my way	pardon, M / M / M, j'ai perdu mon chemin
excuse me, I am lost	pardon, M / M / M, je me suis égaré
excuse me ... could you direct me to ... ?	pardon, monsieur / madame, pour aller ... ?
from / on the other side of the street	de l'autre côté de la rue
go down / descend	descendez
go straight on	allez / continuez tout droit
go through the door	passez par la porte
go up two floors	montez / descendez de deux étages
go up / climb (street, hill, steps)	montez
have you a road map?	avez-vous une carte routière?
how can I get there?	comment puis-je m'y rendre?
how far are you going?	jusqu'où allez-vous?
how far is it to ... ?	quelle est la distance d'ici à ... ?
how far is it to the nearest ... ?	à combien d'ici est le / la ... le / la plus proche?
how far is it to ... ?	combien y a-t-il jusqu'à ... ?
how far is X from the railway station?	X est à combien de la gare SNCF?
how long will it take me to get to ... ?	combien de temps vais-je mettre pour aller à ... ?
how many minutes will it take on foot?	j'en ai pour combien de minutes à pied?
I'll go with you	je vous accompagne
I'm not from around here	je ne suis pas du coin
I'm on foot	je suis à pied
in which direction is ... ?	dans quelle direction se trouve ... ?
is ... here?	est-ce bien ici qu'on trouve ... ?
is it far from here?	est-ce loin d'ici?
is it far to Paris?	c'est loin pour aller à Paris?
is it far?	c'est loin?
is there a ... near here?	y a-t-il un / une ... près d'ici?

is this the way to the station?	c'est bien le chemin de la gare?
it is not the right office	ce n'est pas le bon bureau
it is on the corner	ça fait le coin
it is three minutes from here	c'est à trois minutes d'ici
it will take you ten minutes on foot	vous en avez pour 10 minutes à pied
near to / next to …	près de / à côté de …
not at all / don't mention it	de rien
on the banks of / on the side of …	au bord de …
one way street	rue à sens unique fs
pass in front of	vous passez devant
pedestrian precinct	zone piétonne fs
picnic area	aire de pique-nique
take the fourth on the left	prenez le quatrième à gauche

to the post office / police station / town hall	à la poste / au commissariat / à la mairie
please	s'il vous plaît
turn	tournez
turn left / right	prenez à gauche / droite
under	au-dessous de
walk / drive alongside	longez
what is the quickest way to the village?	quel est le chemin le plus court pour aller au village?
when you reach the Café de la Paix	quand vous arriverez au Café de la Paix
where are the toilets?	où sont les toilettes?
which road do I take?	quelle route est-ce que je dois prendre?
would you repeat that please?	voulez-vous répéter svp?
you go in front of ...	vous passez devant ...
you should have turned right / left	il fallait tourner à droite / gauche

Garage

Vehicle Accessories

15 Watt	15 Watts
accelerator pedal	pédale d'accélération fs
air filter	filtre à air ms
all models	tous modèles mpl
alternator	alternateur ms
antifreeze	antigel ms
ask the salesman	consultez le vendeur
axle	essieu ms
bearing	coussinet ms
belt	courroie fs
bleed the brakes	purger les freins
bolt	boulon ms
bonnet	capot ms
brake disc	plaquette de freins fs
brake fluid	liquide de freins ms
brake pipe	flexible de freins ms
brakes	freins mpl
bubble pack	blister ms
bumper	pare-chocs ms
car manual	revue technique fs
car washing kit	kit de lavage
carburettor	carburateur ms
carburettor jets	gicleurs de carburateur mpl
chamois leather	éponge chamoisée fs
choke	starter ms
cleaning pad	tampon d'essuyage
clutch	embrayage ms
clutch lining	garniture fs d'embrayage
courtesy light	plafonnier ms
crankshaft	vilebrequin ms
cylinder	cylindre ms
cylinder size	cylindrée fs
dashboard	tableau de bord ms
(defective) fuel pump	pompe à essence (défectueuse) fs
defrosting spray	dégivrant ms
diesel engine oil	lubrifiant pour moteur diésel ms
diesel filter	filtre à gasoil ms
diesel preheat plugs	bougies de préchauffage diésel

differential	différentiel ms
dipstick	jauge d'huile fs
disc brake	frein à disque ms
distilled water	eau distillée fs
distributor	distributeur ms
door	portière fs
door protector	butoir de porte ms
drum brake	frein à tambour
elastic strap	sandow de sécurité ms
emergency fan belt	courroie de secours fs
estate car	break ms
exhaust	échappement ms
exhaust pipe	tuyau d'échappement ms
extension cable	câble prolongateur
extinguisher	extincteur ms
fan	ventilateur ms
fan belt	courroie de ventilateur fs
fitting charge	forfait montage ms
fittings for exhausts	accessoires échappement ms
fog lamp	feu anti-brouillard ms
fog light	phare ms antibrouillard
folder	dépliant ms
foot brake	frein à pied ms
foot pump	pompe à pied fs
front nearside headlamp	feu avant droit ms
front / rear axle unit	train avant / arrière ms
fuel filter	filtre à essence ms
fuel supply fault	défaut d'alimentation ms
fuel tank	réservoir ms
fuse	fusible ms
fuse box	boîte à fusibles fs
gear lever	levier des vitesses ms
gearbox	boîte de vitesses fs
gears	vitesses fpl
glue	colle fs
hand brake	frein à main ms
handle	poignée fs
head gasket	joint de culasse ms
heating	chauffage ms
heavy duty / no maintenance	batterie forte puissance / sans entretien fs
high level stop light	feu anti-collision ms
high performance diesel engines	moteurs diésel performants mpl

horn	klaxon / avertisseur ms
ignition	allumage ms
inspection lamp	baladeuse à enrouleur fs
insulating tape	chatterton ms
jack	cric ms
jubilee clip	collier de serrage ms
leadfree fuel	essence sans plomb fs
lockable filler cap	bouchon antivol ms
locking wheel nuts	antivol des roues ms
main applications	principales affectations fpl
make	marque fs
mineral oil	huile minérale fs
number plate	plaque de police fs
nut	écrou ms
oil change	vidange fs
oil filter	filtre à huile ms
paint aerosol	bombe de peinture fs
permanent cooling fluid	liquide de refroidissement permanent ms
piston ring	bague de piston fs
plug	bougie fs
points	vis platinées fpl
puncture	crevaison fs
radio fitting kit (electrical)	faisceau auto-radio ms
rear axle	pont arrière ms
rear fog lamp	brouillard arrière ms
rear view mirror	rétroviseur ms
reflector	réflecteur ms
reline brakes	changer les garnitures fs de freins
removable anti theft drawer	tiroir extractible antivol ms
replacement glass	glace de rechange fs
reverse warning	alarme de recul fs
reversing	marche arrière fs
reversing light	feu de recul ms
right headlamp	projecteur droit ms
roof rack	porte-bagages ms
saloon	berline fs
scraper	raclette fs
seat	siège ms
seat cover	housse fs
shock absorber	amortisseur ms
side light	feu de position ms
silencer	silencieux ms

spare part	pièce de rechange fs / pièce détachée
spare tyre	pneu de secours ms
spare wheel	roue de rechange fs
speedometer	indicateur ms de vitesse
spring	ressort ms
stall	caler
starter	démarreur ms
steering wheel	volant ms
stud	cabochon ms
suitable for catalysers	compatible avec les pots catalytiques
suits the following vehicles	convient aux véhicules suivants
sump	carter ms
sun roof	toit ouvrant ms
sun visor (adhesive)	film solaire ms
suspension	suspension fs
synthetic oil	huile de synthèse fs
tappets	poussoir ms
telescopic wheel nut spanner	clé démonte-pneus télescopique fs
theft lock	canne à clé fs
thermostat	thermostat ms
to have a light not working	avoir une lampe hors d'usage
tyre inflator (foam)	aérosol dépannage crevaison ms
universal joint	cardan ms
valve (engine)	soupape fs
vehicle with gutters	véhicule à gouttières ms
weld, solder	souder
wheel cylinder	cylindre roue ms
wheel trim	enjoliveur ms
window	glace fs
windscreen	pare-brise ms
windscreen washer	lave-glace ms
windscreen wiper	essuie-glaces ms
windscreen wiper blade	balai d'essuie-glace ms
wire strippers	pince à dénuder fs

Repairs / Servicing

can I garage the car here?	puis-je garer la voiture ici ?
can you check the brake fluid?	pouvez-vous vérifier le liquide des freins?
can you make a temporary repair?	pouvez-vous faire une réparation temporaire?
can you repair it?	pouvez-vous la réparer?
can you replace the wiper blades?	pouvez-vous changer les balais des essuie-glace?

can you send someone to look at it?	pouvez-vous envoyer quelqu'un pour l'examiner?
can you send someone to tow it away?	pouvez-vous envoyer quelqu'un pour la remorquer?
do I need a new inner tube?	ai-je besoin d'une nouvelle chambre à air?
have you a breakdown service?	avez-vous un service de dépannage?
how long will it take?	combien de temps faudra-t-il?
how long will the repair take?	combien de temps prendra la réparation?
how long will the repairs take?	combien faudra-t-il pour les réparations?
how long will you be?	combien de temps vous faudra-t-il?
how much will it cost?	combien cela coûtera-t-il?
I am on the road from ... to ...	je suis sur la route de ... à ...
I have electrical / mechanical problems	j'ai des ennuis électriques / mécaniques
I have lost my ignition key	j'ai perdu ma clef de contact
I would like an itemized bill	je voudrais une facture détaillée
I would like it as soon as possible	je la voudrais le plus tôt possible
in three hours	dans trois heures
is it serious?	est-ce grave?
is there a mechanic?	y a-t-il un mécanicien?
it is an automatic and cannot be towed	c'est une automatique et on ne peut pas la remorquer
it is not running properly	elle ne marche pas bien
it needs charging	il faut la recharger
it will take two days	cela prendra trois jours
may I use your phone?	puis-je utiliser votre téléphone?
my battery is flat	ma batterie est déchargée
my car has broken down near here	ma voiture est en panne tout près d'ici
my car has broken down	ma voiture est en panne
my car won't start	ma voiture ne démarre pas
my exhaust has dropped off	j'ai perdu mon pot d'échappement
near kilometre post ...	près de la borne kilométrique ...
please adjust the brakes / steering / lights	veuillez régler les freins / la direction / les phares
please service the car	veuillez faire les vidanges et un graissage complet
the air conditioning does not work	la climatisation ne marche pas
the bodywork is damaged	la carrosserie est endommagée
the carburettor needs regulating	le carburateur a besoin d'un réglage
the engine is misfiring / knocks	le moteur tourne mal / cogne
the engine is not firing properly	l'allumage est faible
the engine is overheating	le moteur chauffe
the engine misfires before stalling	le moteur a des ratés avant de caler

the lock is broken / jammed	la serrure est cassée / bloquée
the oil needs changing	il faut faire la vidange de l'huile
the radiator is leaking	il y a une fuite au radiateur
the transmission fluid level	le niveau de la boîte
the valve / the radiator leaks	la valve / le radiateur fuit
there is a fuel leak	il y a une fuite de carburant
there is a noise	il y a un bruit
there is a petrol / oil leak	il y a une fuite d'essence / d'huile
there is a puncture	il y a un pneu crevé
there is a smell of burning rubber	ça sent le caoutchouc brûlé
there is a smell of petrol	il y a une odeur d'essence
there is a squeak	il y a quelque chose qui grince
here is something wrong in ...	il y a quelque chose qui ne va pas dans ...
this tyre is flat	ce pneu est à plat
to start the engine	mettre le moteur en marche
tubeless	sans chambre à air
wash and grease the car please	lavage et graissage svp
we can make a temporary repair	nous pouvons faire une réparation provisoire
we have to send for the parts	nous devons faire venir les pièces
we haven't got the necessary parts	nous n'avons pas les pièces nécessaires
when will my car be ready?	quand puis-je venir prendre ma voiture?
where are you?	où êtes-vous?
where is there a ... agent?	où y a-t-il une agence ...
where is your car?	où est votre voiture?
will you accept this AA voucher?	accepteriez-vous ce bon de l'Association Automobile?
will you replace this faulty plug?	voulez-vous remplacer cette bougie défectueuse?
will you tow it in?	voulez-vous la remorquer?

Filling Station

Attended Service   Ici On Vous Sert

65

... francs worth of premium please	pour ... francs de super svp
... litres of ordinary / premium	... litres d'essence ordinaire / de super
at the rear	en arrière
can you clean the car please?	pouvez-vous nettoyer la voiture svp?
could you clean the windscreen please?	pouvez-vous nettoyer le pare-brise svp?
could you lend me a can?	pouvez-vous me prêter un bidon?
fill it up please	le plein svp
have you a bulb of this size?	avez-vous une ampoule de cette grandeur?
how much is petrol a litre?	combien vaut le litre d'essence?
I have run out of petrol	je suis en panne d'essence
is there a garage open all night?	y a-t-il un garage ouvert toute la nuit?
please check the oil and water	vérifiez l'huile et l'eau svp
the pressure is 2.3 front and 2.5 rear	c'est 2,3 à l'avant et 2,5 à l'arrière
the pressure should be ... kilos per square centimeter in the front / rear	la pression doit être ... kilos par centimètre en avant / arrière
will you check the tyre pressure?	voulez-vous vérifier la pression des pneus?

4

The camp site

There are far more sites in France than in the UK. It is quite feasible to drive along your chosen route until you happen across one. They are generally well signposted, frequently at the approach to a village or town and often with their star rating. Many localities have several sites, private and municipal. Municipal sites are usually much better value.

- The booking unit is usually 24 hours, midday to midday.

- If you have a wide motor- or towed van or double-axled van, beware that many sites, even municipal, are now making new regulations excluding double-axled vans. They are also narrowing the entrances to their sites. The reason often given is that the ground is unstable! Coincidentally this also prevents access for **"les Gens de la Route"** (Travellers) as they are called!

- Many sites have facilities for the disabled, but do check before booking in. No-one will refuse you a look-around **provided you ask first!**

- Barbecues may well be strictly prohibited. Read the signs or ask beforehand. Fire risk can be extreme. Some sites only have communal barbecues but you will need to get in early!

- The continental, or "hole-in-the-ground" toilet may well be the only type. Check first if this bothers you or you find them difficult. Many French people's first concern is the **Bloc Sanitaire**! They will investigate this before anything else and its suitability will decide whether a booking is made.

- Showers and toilets can be mixed or not labelled.

- Urinals may be "al fresco". Some pitches may be right next to them. On some sites access to the women's toilets may be via the men's.

- Washing-up and clothes washing areas are often separate and strictly delineated. Hot water may not be available in both.

- Hot water may not be available all day especially out of season.

- Some sites sell **"jetons"** or tokens for showers, ironing, washing machines etc. These are usually refundable if unused.

- If a particular site is crucial to your plans and you have not booked, phone ahead to check if it is open. It is not unknown for some sites to claim certain open seasons in the Guides and for the owner to shut up shop, particularly out of the High Season!

- Other than in the **Grandes Vacances** in July and August, site facilities can be very limited. This is true even of May, June and the beginning of September. There may be no visiting shops, open pools, takeaways or entertainment.

- Prices must be displayed at the entrance to the site.

- Site offices may well be closed for a three hour lunch, particularly in the South. In this case there may be a notice telling you to site yourself and report later to the office.

- Some little rural sites will have no resident **Gardien(ne).** S/he will come around once or twice a day to register you and collect your fees. There is often an "honesty box" for those who are unable to wait.

- Most sites apart from those close to the Channel Ports, will have a barrier which closes at 2200 and re-opens at varying times in the morning. Check if you need to make an early departure.

- Many sites require 24 hours notice of departure.

- Some sites have a "quarantine" park for very early / late arrivals and departures

- Prior payment may be demanded for very short stays.

- The Camping Carnet is compulsory on some sites - it gives the owner insurance against damage and non-payment. Motoring Organizations and the Camping Clubs can provide it.

- Beware that your passport may be demanded as a deposit if you have no Carnet. This can be inconvenient if you need to go to the bank or if stopped by the police, since the carrying of ID is compulsory.

- If you are able, check the supply polarity. It is often reversed! If it is, you can swap over the wires in your lead - **but only if you know what you are doing**! A quicker, safer alternative is to carry an extra lead which is already made up with the opposite polarity.

- Very many campsite staff, despite popular belief, **do not** speak English! - even in places like Cherbourg!

- Water and electricity points are often on the same bollard!

- Remember that not all water is drinkable. Non-drinking water is labelled "**eau non potable**".

- Don't forget your continental adapter if you need electrical hookup. Many French sites are not yet equipped with the eurostandard blue sockets. It is as well to take a short length of cable with a normal French plug at one end and a eurosocket at the other.

- Some sites are crammed full of static caravans in varying states of dilapidation. This can be very depressing in the off-season. Beware too of the very long and often frayed extension leads on these sites. The Caravan Club Guide advises where statics are a feature.

- Chemical Toilet Disposal Points are uncommon since French caravans tend not to have loos and sites provide them of course. Ask where to dispose of waste at the **Accueil / Bureau**. Generally it has to be (carefully!) tipped into the normal toilet.

- Some sites do not provide toilet paper.

- At cleaning times or in Low Season, Men and Women's facilities may be closed alternately or be temporarily unisex.

- Out of season, beware the tree stump lurking in the grass!

Asking for what you want (en français!)

Arrival at the campsite

a bigger pitch	un emplacement plus grand
a wider pitch	un emplacement plus large
a flatter pitch	un emplacement plus plat
a pitch for … nights	un emplacement pour … nuits
are the pitches numbered?	les emplacements, sont-ils numérotés?
are there any messages for me?	y a-t-il des messages pour moi?
are they refundable?	ils sont remboursables?
arrival date	date d'arrivée
as far as possible from the road	aussi loin que possible de la route
at what time do you open the barrier?	à quelle heure ouvrez-vous la barrière?
at what time?	à quelle heure?
bakery	une boulangerie
breadshop	un dépôt de pain
cakeshop / confectioner's	une pâtisserie
can I have it?	je peux le prendre?
can I see the pitch?	puis-je voir l'emplacement?
can one swim in the river?	peut-on nager dans la rivière?
can you … ?	pouvez-vous … ?
car / motorbike	une voiture / moto
caravan	une caravane
departure date	la date de départ
do I have to order bread?	faut-il commander le pain?
do I have to pay extra for showers?	y a-t-il un supplément pour les douches?
do I have to pay the day before departure?	faut-il régler la veille du départ?
do you allow double axled caravans?	acceptez-vous les caravanes à double essieu?
do you close the barrier at night?	fermez-vous la barrière la nuit?
do you need a deposit?	y a-t-il une caution?
do you need my carnet?	vous faut-il mon carnet camping?
do you sell English newspapers?	vendez-vous les journaux anglais?
do you want me to settle the bill now?	voulez-vous que je règle la facture maintenant?
does the baker / butcher / fishmonger call?	le boulanger / le boucher / le marchand de poissons passe-t-il?

electric iron	un fer à repasser
for one / two / three	pour une / deux / trois personne(s)
has the weather been good?	a-t-il fait beau ?
have you ... ?	avez-vous ... ?
have you a pitch for one night?	auriez-vous un emplacement pour une nuit?
have you a pitch for several nights?	auriez-vous un emplacement pour plusieurs nuits?
have you any brochures on the town?	avez-vous des dépliants sur la ville?
have you any fresh milk?	avez-vous du lait frais?
have you any ice?	avez-vous de la glace?
here is my carnet	voici mon carnet
here is my passport	voici mon passeport
how far away is the village / town?	le village est à combien de kilomètres d'ici?
how much are they?	combien coûtent-ils?
how much is it?	cela s'élève à combien?
hypermarket	un hypermarché / une grande surface
I don't want electricity	je ne veux pas de branchement
I have no awning	je n'ai pas d'auvent
I would like ...	je voudrais ...
I would like a shadier spot	je voudrais un emplacement plus à l'ombre
I would like a sunnier spot	je voudrais un emplacement plus au soleil
I would like to book in	c'est pour l'inscription
I'd like a token for the washing machine	je voudrais un jeton pour la machine à laver
I'd like play table tennis	je voudrais jouer au ping-pong
in the vicinity	dans les environs
is it alright to use a barbecue?	les barbecues, sont-ils permis?
is that pitch booked?	cet emplacement-là, est-il réservé?
is there any mail for me?	y a-t-il du courrier pour moi?
is it card or coin operated?	elle est à carte où à pièces?
is there a bank in the village?	y a-t-il une banque dans le bourg?
is there a cash machine?	y a-t-il un guichet automatique?
is there a deposit for the key?	y a-t-il une caution sur la clé?
is there a disco?	y a-t-il une disco?
is there a food shop in the village?	y a-t-il une alimentation dans le bourg?
is there a Games Room?	y a-t-il une Salle de Jeux?
is there a Laundry Room?	y a-t-il une salle à linge?
is there a post office nearby?	y a-t-il un PTT dans les environs?
is there a swimming pool?	y a-t-il une piscine?
is there a Tourist Office?	y a-t-il un Syndicat d'Initiatives?
is there a TV Room?	y a-t-il une salle TV?
is there an extra charge for an awning?	y a-t-il un supplément pour l'auvent?
is there entertainment laid on?	y a-t-il de l'animation?
is there hot water for washing up?	y a-t-il de l'eau chaude dans les bacs à laver la vaisselle?

level pitch	un emplacement plat
may I have a token for the showers?	puis-je avoir un jeton pour les douches?
may I park the car next to the tent?	puis-je garer ma voiture à côté de la tente?
may I put this in your fridge?	puis-je mettre ceci dans votre frigo?
may I use a barbecue?	les barbecues sont autorisés?
are open fires allowed?	les feux ouverts, sont-ils autorisés?
may I? (eg taking a brochure)	vous permettez?
motor caravan	un camping-car
my car will not start	je ne peux pas faire démarrer ma voiture
my name is ...	je m'appelle ...
near the river	près de la rivière
no double axled caravans	interdit aux caravanes à deux essieux
one adult	un adulte
one child	un / une enfant
one night	une nuit
pitch near the toilet block	un emplacement près des sanitaires
does the baker call?	le boulanger passe-t-il?
does the fishmonger call?	le marchand de poissons passe-t-il?
probable departure date	la sortie prévue
quiet corner	un coin tranquille
shaded pitch	un emplacement ombragé
shall I pay now?	je règle tout de suite?
shall I pitch anywhere?	puis-je m'installer n'importe où?
sheltered from the wind	à l'abri du vent
site manager	le régisseur
sorry to bother you	je m'excuse de vous déranger
swimming forbidden	baignade interdite

tent	une tente
the chemical toilet emptying point	le point vidange pour les WC chimiques

the circuit breaker has tripped	le disjoncteur a déclenché
there are three of us	nous sommes trois
there are two of us	nous sommes deux
there is no electricity	il y a une panne d'électricité
two children under seven	deux enfants de moins de sept ans
under the trees	sous les arbres
water supply	un point d'eau
we would like ...	nous voudrions ...
what do you charge for ...	quel est le tarif pour ...
what electrical apparatus can I use?	quels appareils électriques puis-je utiliser?
what is the current rating of the electrical supply?	c'est combien d'ampères?
what is the forecast?	quelles sont les prévisions de la météo?
what time is it open?	à quelle heure s'ouvre-t-il / elle?
when do I have to pay?	quand faut-il régler?
when is the bank / office open?	quelles sont les heures d'ouverture de la banque / du bureau?
when is the postal collection?	la levée du courrier est à quelle heure?
when is the postal delivery?	la distribution du courrier est à quelle heure?
where are the dustbins?	où sont les poubelles?
where can I buy charcoal?	où peut-on acheter le charbon de bois?
where can I buy milk?	où peut-on acheter du lait?
where can I buy stamps / postcards?	où peut-on acheter les timbres / cartes-postales?
where can I get a Camping Gaz refill?	où vend-t-on le Camping Gaz?
where can I post letters?	où peut-on poster les lettres?
where do I book in?	où faut-il s'inscrire?
where is ... ?	où est ... ?
where is the chemical disposal point?	où se trouve le W-C chimique / vidoir?
where is the Guardian?	où se trouve le gardien / le responsable?
where is the nearest ... ?	où est le ... le plus proche?
where is the letterbox?	où est la boîte aux lettres?
where is the site office?	où est l'accueil?
where is there a telephone?	où se trouve une cabine téléphonique?
where do I do the dishes?	où fait-on la vaisselle?
where do I do the washing?	où fait-on la lessive?
without electricity	sans branchement / électricité

Departure

and a caravan / tent	et une caravane / tente
... people	... personnes
can I pay by credit card?	puis-je payer par Carte Bleue / carte bancaire?

can I pay by Eurocheque?	puis-je payer par Eurochèque?
can I pay now?	puis-je régler tout de suite?
that makes 3 nights	cela fait trois nuits
do I have to leave by 12?	faut-il partir avant midi?
do I have to notify you 24 hours before I leave?	faut-il vous prévenir 24 heures avant le départ?
I am leaving tomorrow	je vais partir demain
I would like to pay	je voudrais régler la facture
it is the end of the holidays	c'est la rentrée
my name is …	je m'appelle …
no awning	pas d'auvent
no hookup	sans branchement
we arrived on the seventh	nous sommes arrivés le sept
pitch number	emplacement numéro …
we are going home to Great Britain	nous rentrons en Grande Bretagne
we are leaving tomorrow / today	nous partons demain / aujourd'hui
we have not had electricity	nous n'avons pas pris l'électricité
would you do my bill?	voulez-vous bien préparer ma note?
would you give me back my carnet / passport	voulez-vous bien me rendre mon carnet / passeport

Camp site receipt vocabulary

… étoiles	… stars
acompte à déduire	deposit to be deducted
adresse complète	full address
adultes	adults
ampérage	current rating of electric hookup
arrhes versées	deposit paid
arrhes	advance payment
arrivée le:	date of arrival
auvent	awning

Camp site receipt

FÉDÉRATION FRANÇAISE DE CAMPING ET DE CARAVANING
78, rue de Rivoli - 75004 PARIS - Tél. : 16 (1) 42 72 84 08

Nº 00476

CAMPING de _Quillan_ EMPLACEMENT Nº ....

Chef de famille ou Responsable
NOM : _ALLEN_ Prénoms _Richard_

Adresse complète : ....

CODE POSTAL : .... Ville : ....

Nationalité : _GB_ Association : ....

ARRIVÉE LE : _29.06.96_
DÉPART LE : _05.07.96_ Soit : _6_ jours (A)

DÉSIGNATION	NOMBRE	PRIX T.T.C. UNITAIRE	MONTANT JOURNALIER T.T.C.	
			B	C
LOCATION				
FORFAIT DE SÉJOUR				
ADULTES	2	18	36	
ENFANTS MOINS DE 7 ANS				
EMPLACEMENT			18	
ANIMAUX				
ÉLECTRICITÉ				
TAXE DE SÉJOUR				

CACHET DU TERRAIN ET VISA DU GARDIEN

CAMPING MUNICIPAL
La Sapinette ★★★
21, Rue René Delpech
11500 QUILLAN - Tel 68 20 13 52

TOTAL PARTIEL		54
TOTAL JOURNALIER (B + C) = D	=	54
TOTAL T. T. C. (A x D)	=	324,00
dont T.V.A.		16.88
ARRHES	−	
TOTAL A PAYER		324.00

MODE DE PAIEMENT : Cochez la case correspondante

ESPÈCES	CH. BANCAIRE	C. C. P.	EURO CHÈQUE	AUTRES

cachet du terrain	site stamp
campeur	camper
camping-car	motorhome
caravane	caravan
carte d'identité	identity card
caution	deposit
ch. bancaire	cheque
chef de famille	head of family
cochez la case correspondante	tick relevant box
code postal	post code

départ le:	date of departure
dépenses annexes	additional charges
désignation	description
dont TVA	plus VAT
droits de séjour	charges for stay
électricité	hookup
éléments du décompte	breakdown of calculation
emplacement	pitch
en majuscules	please print
enfants jusqu'à 7 ans	children up to 7
enfants moins de 7 ans	children under 7
espèces	cash
facturation	invoicing
fiche renseignements	information slip
forfait de séjour	tariff
forfait hors saison	low season rate
forfait saison	rate for season
garage mort	storage
hors saison	off season
journée famille supplémentaire	family rate - additional day
licence de camping	camping permit
location	hire
matériel roulant	wheeled equipment
mode de paiement	method of payment
montant journalier	daily total
nationalité	nationality
net à payer TTC	net total payable including tax
No minéralogique	vehicle registration
no. d'immatriculation (voiture / moto)	registration number (car / motorbike)
nom	surname
nombre de jours	number of days
nombre de nuits	number of nights
nombre	number (of campers)
par nuit	per night
prénoms	first names
prix TTC unitaire	price per person including all taxes
quittance no.	account no.
reçu la somme de …	received the sum of …
redevances	charges
régisseur	manager
renseignements	information
report total	total brought forward

saison	high season
semaine famille	weekly family rate
soit … jours	ie … days
sommes percues	sums received
sortie prévue	provisional departure date
tarifs nuitée	nightly rate
taxe de séjour	local visitors' tax
tente / toile de tente	tent
total (du) séjour	total for stay
total à payer	total payable
total du séjour	total for stay
total facture	invoice total
total général	total
total journalier	daily total
total partiel	sub-total
véhicule	vehicle
versement en numéraire	sum paid in figures
visa du gardien	guardian's stamp
voiture supplémentaire	additional car

Problems

all my belongings have been stolen	toutes mes affaires ont été volées
can I leave my driving licence in its place?	puis-je laisser mon permis de conduire à sa place?
Fire!	Au Feu!
Help!	Au Secours!
I am so sorry	je suis vraiment désolé
I have no Identity Card	je n'ai pas de Carte d'Identité
I have run out of gas	je suis en panne de gaz

I need my passport for the bank	J'ai besoin de mon passport pour la banque
I need to keep my passport	je dois garder mon passeport
I would like to change pitches	je voudrais changer d'emplacement
I'm sorry	je suis désolé
it barks all night	il aboie toute la nuit
it is making a mess everywhere	il fait ses besoins partout
it should be on a lead	il devrait être tenu en laisse
may I change pitches?	puis-je changer d'emplacements?
the flush is not working	la chasse d'eau ne marche pas
the lights are broken	les lumières ne fonctionnent pas
the shower is flooded	la douche est inondée
the shower is too hot / cold	la douche est trop chaude / froide
the toilet is blocked	le water-closet est bouché
the toilet is overflowing	le W.-C. déborde
the toilets are dirty	les W.-C. sont sales
there a dog which is making a nuisance of itself	il y a un chien qui cause des problèmes
there is a leak	il y a une fuite
there is a mistake on my bill	il y a une erreur sur ma facture
there is no bolt on the shower door	il n'y a pas de verrou à la porte de la douche
there is no hot water	il n'y a pas d'eau chaude
there is no toilet paper	il n'y a pas de papier hygiénique

Greetings / wishes

Cheers!	A la vôtre!
Enjoy the remainder of your holiday	Bonne continuation
Enjoy your meal	Bon appétit
Good evening / Good night	Bonsoir
Good morning / afternoon	Bonjour
How are you ?	Comment allez-vous?
How do you do?	Enchanté(e)
Have a good trip	Bonne Route
This is my wife	Je vous présente ma femme
Enjoy your trip out / walk / drive	Bonne promenade

Things you may hear or read

avez-vous un auvent?	have you an awning?
cela vous arrange?	does that suit you?
c'est possible	that is possible
c'est pour combien de nuits / personnes?	it is for how many nights / people?
c'est pour quoi?	what do you want?
c'est pour une toile de tente?	is it for a tent?
ce n'est pas possible	it is not possible
celui-ci est libre	this one is free
combien d'adultes?	how many adults?
il fallait commander le pain, sinon …	there is no bread unless you have ordered it
il nous reste un seul emplacement	we have only one pitch
installez-vous où vous voudrez	pitch where you like
Interdit aux caravanes à 2 essieux	No double axled caravans
je suis désolé mais …	I am very sorry but …
je vais vous le montrer	I will show you it
je vous accompagne	I will come with you
la clef est consignée	there is a deposit on the key

la marque de votre voiture	the make of your car
Lavage des véhicules interdit	Vehicle washing is forbidden
le numéro d'immatriculation de votre voiture	your car registration number

nous n'avons plus de place	we have no more room
nous sommes complet / on est complet	we are full
on ferme à dix heures	we close at ten
sans branchement	without hookup
suivez-moi	follow me
tous les emplacements sont réservés	all the pitches are booked
veuillez remplir cette fiche	please fill in this slip
Vidoir pour wc chimiques et broyeurs	Disposal point for chemical toilets and waste disposal units
vos enfants, quel âge ont-ils?	how old are your children?
votre carte d'identité / passeport	your ID card / passport
voulez-vous commander du pain?	do you want to order bread?
voulez-vous des jetons pour les douches?	would you like tokens for the showers?
voulez-vous être au bord de la rivière?	would you like to be by the river?
voulez-vous un emplacement ombragé / au soleil?	do you want a shady / sunny pitch?
vous avez réservé?	have you booked?
vous avez un carnet?	have you a carnet?
vous êtes combien?	how many of you are there?
vous signez ici	sign here
vous voulez l'électricité?	do you want electricity?
vous voulez le branchement électrique?	do you want a hookup?
vous vous installez entre les poteaux blancs	park between the white posts

Gate Closure

Many sites, particularly the municipal ones, close the barrier at 10 pm. This can pose a problem for late arrivals or if you go out for the evening, especially in a motor caravan, since you will not be able to use your pitch. Some sites have what they call transit pitches for this purpose and for early departers so as not to disturb the main area out of hours.

Electrical appliances

As already mentioned, many French campsites are not yet equipped with the new Euro standard supply and polarity too can often turn out to be incorrect. The site owners / managers are usually completely unaware of the dangers of reversed polarity and regard any query as an example of quirky "English" customs, to be greeted with, at best, amused tolerance or stoical resignation. Incidentally, all Brits, whether Scots, Welsh, Irish or English are **"les Anglais"** to the majority of French people.

Another problem is the low current ratings. Many sites supply only 2 amps or maybe 5 amps. 10 amps is a rarity. Any attempt to use appliances other than those which fall within the range will of course result in blown or tripped fuses and a not very happy **Gardien**.

Examples of suitable appliances:

Radiateur	Radiator	
Cafetière	Coffee Pot	**2A**
Séchoir	Hairdryer	
Fer à repasser	Iron	

Eclairage	Lighting	
Frigidaire	Fridge	
Fer à friser	Hair tongs / curlers	**5A**
Rasoir électrique	Electric shaver	
Télé	TV (B/W)	

Electric kettles are unusual in France and the supply would certainly not cope with the average 2400 watt British appliance. Camping suppliers in the UK stock kettles rated at 750w which are usable on a 5A supply. The heating time is however quite long. Colour TV's will need 5A.

Radio Stations

- The BBC domestic stations as well as the World Service can be picked up in northern France.

- There are two English language stations in the South of France:

    - Crown Radio 102 retransmits BBC World Service on 108 MHz FM

    - Riviera Radio transmits on 106.3 and 106.5 MHz

5

If things go wrong!

Consulates

If you have problems, remember that the British Consul is not a Travel Agent, rescue service, bank, nursemaid or miracle worker. Contact him / her only in a real emergency, otherwise use the appropriate local organization. (See Emergency Telephone Numbers, Police, Garage services, Car Hire, Medical etc). Most normal emergencies will be dealt with efficiently by your Motoring Organization or Travel Insurer.

What a Consul **can** do

- Issue emergency passports

- Contact relatives and friends and ask them to help you with money or tickets

- Advise on how to transfer funds

- At most posts (in an emergency) advance money against a sterling cheque for up to £100 supported by a banker's card valid for the appropriate amount

- As a last resort, and provided that certain strict criteria are met, make a repayable loan in exceptional circumstances for repatriation to the UK. But there is no law that says the Consul must do this, and the Consul will need to be satisfied that there is absolutely no one else you know who can help

- Help you get in touch with local lawyers, interpreters and doctors

- Arrange for next of kin to be informed of an accident or a death and advise on procedures

- Contact and visit British nationals under arrest or in prison and, in certain circumstances, arrange for messages to be sent to relatives or friends

- Give guidance on organizations experienced in tracing missing persons

- Make representations on your behalf to the local authorities in certain circumstances.

But a Consul **cannot**

- Intervene in court proceedings

- Get you out of prison

- Give legal advice or instigate court proceedings on your behalf

- Get better treatment for you in hospital or prison than is provided for local nationals

- Investigate a crime

- Pay your hotel, legal, medical or any other bills

- Pay for travel tickets for you except in very special circumstances

- Undertake work more properly done by travel representatives, airlines, banks or motoring organizations

- Obtain accommodation, work or a work permit for you

- Formally assist dual nationals in the country of their second nationality.

If you are arrested:

If you commit an offence you must expect to face the consequences. If you are charged with a serious offence, insist on the British consulate's being informed. You will be contacted as soon as possible by a consular officer.

The officer can advise on local procedures, provide access to lawyers, and can insist that you are treated as well as French nationals. But the officer cannot pay for a lawyer for you, cannot put up bail, and cannot get you released as a matter of course.

If you have anything stolen:

If you lose your money, passport or anything else abroad, report it first to the local police and insist on a statement about the loss. (See relevant section) Then contact the Consulate if you still need their help.

If someone dies:

In the case of a fatal accident - or death from whatever cause - get in touch with the Consulate at once. The Consul will help.

Parliament lays down that fees can be charged for some services.

Consular Services:

Paris
British Embassy
35 rue du Faubourg St Honoré
Tel: 01 42 66 91 42

Biarritz
British Consulate
c/o Barclays Bank SA
7 Avenue Edward VII BP98
Tel: 05 59 24 04

Bordeaux
British Consulate General
353 Blvd du President Wilson
Tel: 05 56 42 34 13

Boulogne
British Consulate
c/o Cabinet Barron & Brun
"La Carte" 88-100 Route De Paris, St-Martin-Boulogne
Tel: 03 21 87 16 80

Calais
British Consulate
c/o P&O European Ferries
41 Place d'Armes
Tel: 03 21 96 33 76

Cherbourg
British Consulate
c/o P&O Ferries
Gare Maritime Sud
Tel: 02 33 44 20 13

Dunkirk
British Consulate
c/o Dewulf Cailleret & Fils
(1st Floor) 11 rue des Arbres, BP 1502
Tel: 03 28 66 11 98

Le Havre
British Consulate
Lloyds Register of Shipping
24 Bvd de Strasbourg
Tel: 02 35 42 42 15

Lille
British Consulate General
11 Square Dutilleul
Tel: 03 20 57 87 90

Lyon
British Consulate General
24 rue Childebert
Tel: 04 78 37 59 67

Marseille
British Consulate General
24 Avenue du Prado
Tel: 04 91 53 43 32

Nantes
British Consulate
L'Aumarière, Coueron
Tel: 02 40 63 16 02

Nice
British Consulate
2 rue du Congrès
Tel: 04 93 82 32 04

Paris
British Consulate General
9 Avenue Hoch
Tel: 01 42 66 38 10

St Malo-Dinard
British Consulate
La Hulotte
8 Blvd des Maréchaux
Tel: 02 99 46 26 64

Toulouse
British Consulate
c/o Lucas Aerospace Victoria Centre
Bâtiment Didier Daurat, 20 Chemin de Laporte
Tel: 05 61 15 02 02

Garage servicing

- Garages are obliged to display the hourly labour rates as well as those for different basic services (tax included) outside the garage as well as at the reception desk. There are three hourly rates:

    T1 for usual repairs (puncture, oil change)
    T2 such as carburettor cleaning
    T3 for very specialised repairs

- The "**Ordre de Réparation**", a written document, signed by yourself and the garage mechanic, specifies the exact nature of the repair, the estimated cost and the time to be taken. Make sure you ask for the **"Ordre"**.

Loss of Driving Licence

This must be reported at once to the police or **Gendarmerie** when Form 1 will be issued. (See this chapter.)

Remember too that insurance claims for theft or loss of other items must be supported by a police report. You will have to ask for this as some police officers are unaware that loss of money for example is covered by UK insurance policies, unlike French ones.

Directions for use of the European Accident Statement (Constat amiable d'accident automobile)

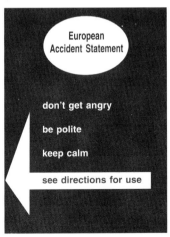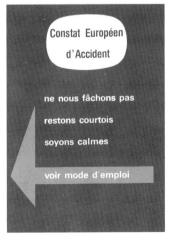

- (It is advisable to keep the form with a ballpoint pen in the glove compartment)

85

- The purpose of the form is to get a statement of the facts of the accident agreed by each driver.

- The foreign driver will have a form identical in every way apart from the language and either may be filled in. (A continental driver may fill in his form in his own language, leaving you to complete your part of his form in English - Check on what the questions mean on your own form).

- It is essential to retain either the original or the carbon copy and to send it to your insurer.

At the accident scene

- Get details of all witnesses. Fill in question 5.

- Complete in ball point pen if possible either the yellow or blue part of the Agreed Statement of Facts. (Check your insurance certificate, Green Card and driving licence details).

- French registered cars carry a small ticket in the windscreen showing that the insurance and **Contrôle Technique** (MOT) are current. The **Certificat d'Assurance** is a useful double check in the case of accident. The last two numbers of the registration plates of a French owned car relate to the **Département**. eg **Yvelines 78** (See Departmental list).

- When sure that the form is accurately completed, both drivers sign it

Remember to:

- Mark clearly on diagram (10) the point of initial impact.

- Put a cross (X) in each relevant square on your side of (12) and indicate the total number of boxes marked with a cross.

- Draw a plan of the accident spot (13) showing all the information requested.

- Take photos of the scene, damage and those involved.

- DO NOT alter the statement of facts after completion.

At home:

- Fill in the Motor Accident Report on the back of the English version of the Agreed Statement of Facts.

- Send both parts at once to your insurer, preferably keeping a photocopy.

- This form can be used even when no other vehicle is involved - for example damage to your own car, theft, fire, injury to third parties.

It may be that you do not have your form to hand, so here are the expressions used on the form in the order in which they occur:

> **constat amiable d'accident automobile.**
> agreed statement of facts on motor vehicle accident.
>
> **Ne constitue pas une reconnaissance de responsabilité mais un relevé des identités et des faits servant à l'accélération du règlement**
> Does not constitute an admission of liability but a summary of identities and of the facts which will speed up the settlement of claims
>
> **à signer obligatoirement par les deux conducteurs.**
> MUST be signed by both drivers.
>
> | | |
> |---|---|
> | lieu ms | place |
> | blessés même légers mpl | injured parties, even if slightly hurt |
> | dégâts matériels mpl | property damage |
> | autres qu'aux véhicules A et B | other than to vehicles A and B |
> | témoins | witnesses |
> | à souligner s'il s'agit d'un passager de A ou B | to be underlined if a passenger of A or B |
> | assuré ms | insured |
> | souscripteur ms | policy holder |
> | voir attest. d.'ass. | see ins. cert. |
> | nom ms | surname |
> | majusc. | caps. |
> | prénom ms | first name |
> | l'assuré peut-il récupérer la TVA afférente au véhicule? | can the Insured recover VAT on the vehicle? |
> | marque fs | make |
> | No d'immatr. (ou de moteur) | registration no (or engine no) |
> | sté d'assurance | ins. co. |
> | no. de contrat | policy no. |
> | agence fs | agent |

courtier ms	broker
no. de carte verte	Green Card no.
attest.	ins. cert.
valable jusqu'au	valid until
les dégâts matériels sont-ils assurés?	is damage to the vehicle insured?
conducteur ms	driver
voir permis de conduire	see driving licence
délivré par	issued by
indiquer par une flèche	indicate by an arrow
le point de choc initial	the point of initial impact
dégâts apparents mpl	visible damage
observations fpl	remarks
circonstances fpl	circumstances
mettre une croix dans chacune des cases utiles	put a cross in each relevant box
pour préciser le croquis	to help explain the plan
en stationnement	parked (at the roadside)
quittait un stationnement	leaving a parking place (at the roadside)
prenait un stationnement	entering a parking place (at the roadside)
sortait d'un parking	emerging from a car park
d'un lieu privé	from private grounds
d'un chemin de terre	from a track
s'engageait dans un parking	entering a car park
s'engageait sur une place à sens giratoire	entering a roundabout or similar
roulait sur une place à sens giratoire	circulating on a roundabout
heurtait l'arrière de l'autre véhicule	striking the rear of the other vehicle
qui roulait dans le même sens	travelling in the same direction
sur la même file	in the same lane
sur une file différente	in a different lane
changeait de file	was changing lanes
doublait	was overtaking
virait à droite / gauche	was turning right / left
reculait	was backing up
empiétait sur la partie de la chaussée réservée	was encroaching on the opposite traffic
à la circulation en sens inverse	lane
venait de droite (dans un carrefour)	was coming from the right (at a junction)
n'avait pas observé un signal de priorité	had not obeyed a right of way sign
indiquer le nombre de cases marquées par	state TOTAL number of boxes marked with a
une croix	cross
croquis de l'accident ms	plan of the accident
préciser	indicate
le tracé des voies	road layout
au moment du choc	at time of impact
les signaux routiers	road signs

If you are unfortunate enough to have an accident and do not have a copy of the European Accident Statement:

- Report the accident to the police - compulsory when there is personal injury or material damage

- Give your name and address and that of your insurance company to the third party

- Show your Green Card

- Do not sign or make or any statement without legal advice. It could invalidate the terms of your insurance

- Take photographs of the accident scene

- Draw a diagram of the accident

- Take the following details :

    - other vehicle(s) and their driver(s) passengers

    - name and address of the other party's insurance company

    - names and details of independent witnesses

    - date and time of the accident

    - estimated speeds

    - condition of the other car(s)

    - weather and road conditions

    - new and existing damage on all cars involved

- Report the accident:

    - to your insurance company

    - to the Insurance Bureau of the country concerned (details on Green Card) as soon as you can but at the latest on return to the UK

What Can I Say?

accident report form	carnet de constat ms
accidents where there are no injuries	cas d'accident sans tiers (lésés)
according to the highway code	selon le code de la route
are you hurt?	vous vous êtes fait mal?
book a motorist	dresser un procès-verbal contre un automobiliste
a breakdown vehicle will come to your assistance	un véhicule de dépannage viendra à votre aide
breakdown service	service de dépannage
breakdown tariffs are fixed	les tarifs de dépannage-remorquage sont homologués
breakdown truck	dépanneuse fs
calm down!	calmez-vous!
can I buy spares for a ... ?	puis-je acheter des pièces détachées pour une ... ?
can I pay at the police station?	puis-je payer au commissariat?
can you give me a push?	pouvez-vous me pousser?
can you give me a tow?	vous pouvez me prendre en remorque?
can you lend us a car?	vous pouvez nous prêter une voiture?
can you repair a flat tyre?	pouvez-vous réparer un pneu crevé?
can you send an ambulance?	pouvez-vous envoyer une ambulance?
can you take me to the nearest garage?	pouvez-vous me conduire au garage le plus proche?
can you tow start me?	vous pouvez me faire démarrer en remorque?
collision waiver	rachat de franchise ms
crash barrier	glissière latérale fs
damage to property	dégâts matériels mpl
don't smoke. There is fuel leaking	ne fumez pas. Il y a de l'essence qui fuit
don't touch him / her	ne le / la touchez pas
driving licence	permis de conduire ms
European Accident Declaration Form	Constat amiable - Déclaration d'accident
fill in the accident report	faire le constat
get the statement signed	faites signer le constat
hand one of the copies to him / her	remettez-lui un des exemplaires
have you an extinguisher?	avez-vous un extincteur?
have your tyres inflated	faites gonfler vos pneumatiques
to the recommended pressure	à la pression préconisée
he accelerated	il a accéléré
he braked hard	il a freiné brutalement
he came out of a side road / street	il est sorti d'une route / rue transversale
he crossed the continuous white line	il a franchi la ligne transversale blanche
he has a possible whiplash injury	il a peut-être une lésion traumatique

he hit the traffic cones	il a heurté les cônes de signalisation
he hit the 2CV	il est rentré dans la 2 CV
he is a witness	il est témoin
he left without explanation	il est parti sans explication
he locked the wheels (in skid)	il a bloqué les roues
he lost control on the bend	il a perdu le contrôle dans le virage
he moved off before the lights had changed	il a démarré avant que les feux aient changé
he overtook on a bend	il a doublé dans un virage
he refused to fill in the report	il a refusé de remplir le constat
he rolled over several times	il a fait plusieurs tonneaux
he skidded	il a dérapé
he stopped suddenly	il s'est arrêté brusquement
he struck the rear of my car	il a percuté l'arrière de ma voiture
he struck the safety barrier	il a heurté la glissière de sécurité
he took the bend at over ... mph	il a pris le virage à une vitesse supérieure à ... km / heure
he took the corner too fast	il a pris le virage trop vite
he was driving much too fast	il roulait beaucoup trop vite
he was driving too close / tailgating	il conduisait trop près / il collait à mes pare-chocs
he was exceeding the speed limit	il commettait un excès de vitesse / il dépassait la vitesse permise
hello, is that the police?	allô, c'est bien la police?
help!	au secours!
here are my insurance details	voici mes pièces d'assurance
here are my name and address	je vous donne mon nom et mon adresse
here is my driving licence	voici mon permis de conduire
here is my Green Card	voici ma Carte Verte
here is my Insurance Certificate	voici ma Carte d'Assurance
here is my policy number	je vous donne mon numéro d'assurance
here is the address of my insurance	voici l'adresse des assureurs
his reversing / stop lights were not working	ses feux de recul / de stop ne marchaient pas
how do I call an ambulance?	comment est-ce que j'appelle une ambulance?
how do I call the police?	comment est-ce que j'appelle la police?
how much is the fine?	quel est le montant de la contravention?
I am injured	je suis blessé(e)
I am insured with ...	je suis assuré(e) auprès de ...
I am out of fuel	je suis en panne sèche
I am out of petrol	je suis en panne d'essence
I am very sorry	je suis désolé(e)
I did not realize	je ne me suis pas rendu compte
I didn't realize there was a speed limit	je ne savais pas que la vitesse était limitée
I didn't see him in my mirror	je ne l'ai pas vu dans mon rétroviseur
I don't feel well	je ne me sens pas bien

I had priority	c'est moi qui avais la priorité
I have collided with ...	ma voiture est entrée en collision avec ...
I have locked myself out	les clés sont enfermées à l'intérieur
I have not had anything to drink	je n'ai rien bu
I want to report an accident	je voudrais signaler un accident
I was only doing 50 kph	je ne roulais qu'à 50km/h
inform the police or Gendarmerie	alertez la Police ou la Gendarmerie
insurance documents	documents d'assurance
insurance policy	contrat d'assurance ms
it is not advisable to move injured people	il est déconseillé de déplacer / bouger les blessés
it is urgent	c'est urgent.
it was a lack of concentration	c'était une faute d'inattention
it was a Peugeot estate / saloon	c'était un break / une berline Peugeot
it was coming up in his blind spot	cela approchait dans son angle mort
it was her right of way	c'était elle qui avait la priorité
jump leads	câbles de démarrage
let's deal with this calmly!	soyons calmes surtout!
let's give him / her mouth to mouth	faisons-lui le bouche à bouche
look at the damage	examiner les dégâts
make a claim	faire une demande d'indemnité
make a sketch of the accident	établir un croquis de l'accident
make sure that ...	assurez-vous que ...
my brakes are faulty	mes freins sont défectueux
my car has been towed away to the pound	ma voiture a été emmenée à la fourrière
my car is badly damaged	ma voiture est très endommagée
my car registration number	le numéro d'immatriculation de ma voiture
my driving licence	mon permis de conduire
my home address is in ... (country)	je suis domicilié(e) en ... (pays)
my licence is at the campsite	mon permis de conduire est au camping
my passenger is in shock	mon passager est commotionné
my windscreen is broken / chipped / cracked	mon pare-brise est brisé / ébréché / fêlé
my windscreen wiper has come off	mon essuie-glace s'est détaché
no excess (insurance)	suppression de la franchise fs
no-one was hurt	personne n'a été blessé
no-one would let me change lanes	personne ne voulait me laisser changer de file
on the A10 motorway	sur l'autoroute A10
on the spot fine	amende avec paiement immédiat fs
one of my lights is smashed	l'un de mes phares est brisé
pedestrian crossing	passage pour piétons ms
pedestrian precinct	Zone Piétonne fs
please call me a taxi	appelez-moi un taxi svp
please sign here	veuillez signer ici svp

point of initial impact	point de choc initial ms
puncture	crevaison fs
put on your hazard flashers	faites fonctionner votre système clignotant "alarme"
remain on the hard shoulder	rester immobilisé sur la bande d'arrêt d'urgence
she fell off her bike	elle est tombée de son vélo
she was not wearing a helmet	elle ne portait pas de casque
show your Certificate of Insurance	présentez spontanément votre attestation d'assurance
slightly injured person	blessé léger ms
someone is injured	il y a quelqu'un blessé
stop here please	arrêtez-vous ici svp
Switch on headlights	Allumez vos Lanternes / Feux / Phares
take the motorway	emprunter l'autoroute
the brakes failed	les freins ont lâché
the car caught fire	la voiture a pris feu
the car in front had stopped	la voiture devant nous était à l'arrêt
the car struck him with its nearside wing	la voiture l'a heurté de son aile droite
the car swerved to avoid the pedestrian	la voiture a fait une embardée pour éviter le piéton
the car swerved	la voiture a fait un écart
the car turned right without signalling	la voiture a tourné à droite sans prévenir
the car was driving too close	la caravane s'est mise à zigzaguer
the driver went through a red light	le conducteur a brûlé le feu rouge
the fast lane	voie rapide fs
the fire brigade is on its way	les pompiers arrivent
the fog was very thick	le brouillard était très épais
the HGV could not brake in time	le poids lourd n'a pu freiner à temps
the maximum permitted speed is …	la vitesse maximale permise est ...
the name of your insurers	nom de votre compagnie d'assurance ms
the near / off side	côté droit / gauche ms
the pedestrian stepped out without looking	le piéton a fait un pas en avant sans regarder
the radiator / sump / petrol tank / battery leaks	le radiateur / carter / réservoir / la batterie fuit
the radiator grill is dented	la calandre est cabossée
the road surface was slippery	la chaussée était glissante
the road was icy	la route était verglacée
the road was not clear	la route n'était pas dégagée
the steering is damaged	la direction est endommagée
the traffic lights were difficult to see / too dim	les feux étaient difficiles à voir / trop pâles / faibles
the traffic lights were not working	les feux ne marchaient pas
the tyre burst	le pneu a éclaté

the wheel rim is damaged	la jante est endommagée
the window is shattered	la glace est brisée
the window will not wind up	je ne peux pas remonter la glace
there are two (seriously) injured	il y a deux blessés (graves)
there has been an accident	il y a eu un accident
there is acid everywhere	il y a de l'acide partout
there is another passenger still trapped	il y a encore un passager bloqué dedans
there was a five car shunt	cinq voitures se sont carambolées
there was mud on the road surface	il y avait de la boue sur la chaussée
third party cover	assurance au tiers illimité fs
to book someone	verbaliser qn.
to get arrested	se faire arrêter
to have hazard flashers on	être en warning
to let the ambulance through	pour laisser passer l'ambulance
tow rope	un câble de remorquage
traffic calming hump	ralentisseur ms
turn left / right	tournez à gauche / droite
tyre tread	bande de roulement fs
tyre walls	flancs du pneu mpl
under-inflated tyre	pneu sous-gonflé ms
until it is repaired	jusqu'à ce qu'elle soit réparée
until someone comes out (breakdown)	jusqu'à ce qu'on vienne me dépanner
we must fill in the accident report	nous devons faire le constat d'accident
what papers do I need?	de quels papiers ai-je besoin?
when will the road be clear?	quand est-ce que la voie sera dégagée?
where am I exactly?	où suis-je exactement?
where can I find a doctor?	où est-ce que je peux trouver un médecin?
where can I phone?	où est-ce que je peux téléphoner?
where do I have to inquire?	où faut-il s'adresser?
where the accident took place	sur les lieux de l'accident
where were you heading?	vous alliez où?
whilst overtaking the lorry	en doublant le camion
windscreen breakage	bris de glace ms
without giving me his details	sans me fournir ses coordonnées
witnesses	témoins mpl
would you repeat that please?	voulez-vous répéter svp?
you were in the wrong after all	c'est vous qui aviez tort après tout
you will have to be breathalysed	vous devez subir l'alcootest
your driving licence / logbook please	votre permis de conduire / carte grise svp
your insurance company	votre compagnie d'assurances
your name and address	votre nom et votre adresse

Car Insurance

Car Insurance cover is compulsory and although the International Insurance Certificate (Green Card, or European Cover as some insurance companies are now calling it) is not required in France, it is the best proof of insurance cover, being recognized by the police and other authorities. It is also vital if fully comprehensive cover is to be maintained whilst in Europe. Regardless of your cover in the UK, only minimum Third Party cover is in force in the absence of a Green Card. It is sufficient to have applied for the card; it need not be in your possession, although as stated above, is useful proof. It is **vital** to inform your insurance company when applying for the Green Card if you will be towing and to give full details.

The **AA** and **RAC** provide accident insurance and breakdown service.

Europ Assistance (252 High Street, Croydon CR0 1NF) Tel: (0181) 680 1234 also has special policies for motorists.

Green Flag National Breakdown has an annual cover which is particularly useful to people travelling frequently abroad. Enquiries about membership and cover Tel: (0800) 800 600.

Emergency Telephone Numbers (FREE) - (Numéros Verts):	
• **Police**	Tel: 17
• **Informations** - (Directory Enquiries)	Tel: 12
• **SAMU** - (Medical / ambulance)	Tel: 15
• **Sapeurs-Pompiers** - (Fire Brigade)	Tel: 18

95

Police

It is essential to report any loss of ID or driving licence in case you are stopped by the police, as French law requires ID (and driving licence if applicable) to be carried by all adults at all times. A document will then be issued to cover this situation.   (See Form 2)

Police Advice for Avoiding Street Crime

When parking:

- Lock steering.

- Close all windows.

- Never leave anything on view.

- Avoid parking in dark isolated spots.

- Never leave car with engine running or the key in ignition.

When on foot:

- Beware of pickpockets.

- Carry handbags etc on the side of the pavement nearer the wall and do not walk near the kerb.

- Never carry large sums of money.

- Keep all bags closed and never leave purses on top of shopping.

- Never leave belongings unsupervised.

Remember! In the event of loss, damage or theft a police report must be obtained for subsequent insurance claims purposes. It is much easier done on the spot than by letter on your return!

Lost Property Offices will notify you if items are subsequently found. (See Form 3)

can you give me a copy of the report for my insurance company?	pouvez-vous me faire une copie du p.v. pour ma compagnie d'assurance?
credit cards	cartes de crédit
handbag	sac à main ms
he ran off towards the town centre	il s'est sauvé dans la direction du centre ville
he threatened me with a knife	il m'a menacé d'un couteau
he was a young man of about twenty	c'était un jeune homme d'une vingtaine d'années
here are the numbers	en voici les numéros
I didn't notice straight away	je ne m'en suis pas aperçu tout de suite
I have already telephoned the bank to cancel them	j'ai déjà téléphoné à la banque pour les annuler
I have been attacked	j'ai été agressé(e)
I have lost my travellers' cheques	j'ai perdu mes chèques de voyage
I lost it in town	je l'ai perdu(e) en ville
I lost it this morning / afternoon / yesterday	je l'ai perdu ce matin / cet après-midi / hier
I must have dropped it / them without noticing	j'ai dû le / la / les laisser tomber sans m'en apercevoir
I noticed it after a few minutes	je m'en suis aperçu au bout de quelques minutes
I noticed when I came out of the supermarket	je m'en suis rendu compte quand je suis sorti du supermarché
I suppose no-one has handed in a ... ?	on ne vous aurait pas remis un / une ... ?
I want to report the loss of my...	je voudrais signaler la perte de ...
I was robbed	on m'a volé
I wish to report a loss	je voudrais faire une déclaration de perte
I would like to report a theft / loss	je voudrais signaler un vol / une perte
it is not mine	ce n'est pas le mien / la mienne
it was locked	il / elle était fermé(e)

mine is smaller etc	le mien est plus petit etc
mine looks like it but …	le mien / la mienne lui ressemble mais …
money	argent ms
morning / afternoon	matin / après-midi
my car has been towed away	ma voiture a été enlevée
my caravan has been broken into	on a cambriolé ma caravane
my (hand) bag was snatched by a young man	un jeune homme m'a arraché mon sac (à main)
my insurance company	ma compagnie d'assurance
someone has smashed my car window	on a brisé la glace de ma voiture
someone has stolen my camera	on a volé mon appareil photo
someone mugged me in the street	quelqu'un m'a agressé dans la rue
someone must have stolen it from me in town	quelqu'un a dû me le voler en ville
that one is bigger	celui / celle-là est plus grand(e)
the door / the boot lock has been forced	on a forcé la portière / la serrure du coffre
the other one must have taken my wallet	l'autre a dû prendre mon porte-feuille
there has been an accident	il y a eu un accident
they are denominations of ten and twenty pounds	ce sont des coupures de 10 et de 20 livres
they are Midland Bank sterling cheques	ce sont des chèques en livres sterling de la Banque Midland
traveller's cheques	chèques de voyage
unfortunately I have also lost my bank cards	malheureusement j'ai perdu aussi mes Cartes Bancaire
wallet	porte-monnaie ms

It is an offence under French law not to go to the assistance of a person in danger.

Example of form to be filled in at Gendarmerie as evidence of loss of document eg Driving Licence, ID Card, Passport

CERFA

N° 20-3248

IMPORTANT

Déclaration de perte / de vol de pièces d'identité

Ce document ne peut constituer un duplicata de pièces d'identité.

Il tient lieu de permis de conduire pendant un délai de 2 mois au plus à dater de la déclaration.

(Article R137 du Code de la Route)

Ecrire au stylo à bille en MAJUSCULES d'imprimerie. Ex. DUPONT

1. Déclarant

Nom_____

(pour les femmes, écrire le nom de jeune fille)

Epouse ou veuve de_____

(nom et prénom du mari)

Prénoms_____

(dans l'ordre de l'état civil)

Fils ou Fille de_____

et de_____

Date de naissance | | | | Lieu_____ + |.......|

(commune, département: Paris, Lyon, Marseille, préciser l'arrondissement.) +

Domicile habituel_____

(rue, N°, commune, lieu dit, département)

Pour les personnes de passage_____

(adresse actuelle)

2. Caractéristiques du ou des documents

Carte Nationale d'Identité   Passeport   Permis de conduire

N°:_____

Délivrée le_____

Par:_____

3. Eléments sur la disparition du ou des documents

Date et lieu_____

Circonstances_____

Toute fausse déclaration est passible des peines prévues par l'article 154 du code pénal

Signature du déclarant

Fait à

Le

_____

Partie réservée à l'administration

Autorité recevant En cas de vol:

la déclaration

P.V. N°:

Sceau   Etabli le:

Par:

Exemplaire à remettre au déclarant

Translation of form to be filled in at Gendarmerie as evidence of loss / theft of document eg Driving Licence, ID Card, Passport

CERFA

N° 20-3248

IMPORTANT

Statement of loss / theft of ID

This form is not a duplicate ID card.

It serves as a replacement Driving Licence for a maximum of 2 months from the date of the report of loss.

(Article R137 of the Highway Code)

Use ballpoint pen Print entries. Example DUPONT

1. Person declaring loss

Surname_____

(in case of married woman, maiden name)

Wife or widow of_____

(husband's surname and first name)

Given names_____

(in same order as Birth Certificate)

Son or Daughter of_____

and of_____

Date of Birth | | | | Place_____ + |........|

(Town, county: for cities give district.) +

Home address_____

(street, town, county)

For people in transit_____

(present address)

_____

2. Nature of document(s) lost

ID Card Passport Driving Licence

No:_____ _____

Date of issue_____

by:_____

3. Note of circumstances of loss

Date and Place_____

Circumstances_____

Any false declaration is punishable under the provisions of Article 154 of the penal code

Signature of person making statement

At (place)
Date

_____

For office use only
official receiving declaration In the case of theft:

Statement. N°:

Stamp   Statement taken:

By:

Copy for person making statement

Declaration of loss of documents

Légion de Gendarmerie de Basse Normandie à Caen

Form 2

L'Aigle,
le 3 NOVEMBRE 1998

GROUPEMENT DE L'ORNE
COMPAGNIE DE MORTAGNE-au-PERCHE

BRIGADE DE L'AIGLE
61 Rue Porte RABEL
61300 L'AIGLE

Tél: 02.24.00.17.78

A T T E S T A T ION:
OB J E T : Perte de documents bancaires, administratifs et de numéraires.

Nous soussigné, Gendarme CONDE, Gaëlle
de la Compagnie de MORTAGNE - AU - PERCHE, en résidence à L'AIGLE.

Atteste que : ALLEN, Richard

Profession :

Demeurant : XXXX YYYY à HAMPSHIRE (Angleterre).
S'est présenté à notre unité le : 3 MARS 1998
et a déclaré avoir été victime de la perte de 3 cartes bancaires MIDLAND, Mastercard et
EUROCHEQUES, compte n° ZZZZZZZZZZZ, de son permis de conduire, d'une télécarte et de NNN
livres sterling. Fait commis entre hier soir, vers 18 heures, dans le Métro de Paris et ce matin, à l'Hôtel
Beausoleil de L'AIGLE (61300).
Le déclarant est informé que quiconque aura sciemment utilisé ou fait usage d'une attestation ou d'un
certificat de faits matériellement inexistants ou a modifié une attestation ou un certificat originairement
sincère sera puni des peines prévues
par l'Article 161 du Code Pénal

La personne concernée:

(Signature)   SCEAU

103

Translation of Declaration of loss of documents

Légion de Gendarmerie de Basse Normandie à Caen

L'Aigle,
3rd November 1998

GROUPEMENT DE L'ORNE
COMPAGNIE DE MORTAGNE-au-PERCHE

BRIGADE DE L'AIGLE
61 Rue Porte RABEL
61300 L'AIGLE

Tél: 02.24.00.17.78

Declaration:

Subject : Loss of bank and administrative documents and cash.

We the undersigned, Gendarme CONDE, Gaëlle
of the Compagnie de MORTAGNE - AU - PERCHE, at L'AIGLE.

Attest that : ALLEN, Richard

Profession :

Home address : XXXX YYYY à HAMPSHIRE (Angleterre).

presented himself at our police station on 3rd NOVEMBER 1998 and stated that he had suffered the loss of 3 bank cards MIDLAND, Mastercard and EUROCHEQUE, Account n° ZZZZZZZZZZZ, his driving licence, a Phonecard et de NNN pounds sterling. This happened between yesterday evening 6 pm, in the **Paris Métro** and this morning, at the **Hôtel Beausoleil** of **L'AIGLE** (61300).

The complainant is informed that anyone who knowingly has used or uses a statement or certified declaration of untrue facts or has changed an originally correct statement or a certified declaration will be subject to penal action as provided for in **Article 161** of the **Code Pénal.**

Complainant:

(Signature)   Stamp

Lost Property Notification

DIRECTION DE LA CIRCULATION DES
TRANSPORTS ET DU COMMERCE   Réf. O.T.:012089

4ème Bureau - Objets Trouvés   PARIS le 21/11/1998
36 rue des Morillons
75732 PARIS CEDEX 15

Tél: 01 45 31 98 11

Ouvert sans interruption lundi et mercredi 8h30 - 17h mardi et jeudi 8h30 - 20h
vendredi 8h30 - 17h30 juillet et août 8h30 - 17h Métro CONVENTION Bus 89, PC, 62

MR: ALLEN Richard
XXXXXX   XX
YYYYY
GRANDE BRETAGNE

Monsieur,

Je vous informe que des objets ou des documents portant vos nom et adresse ont été déposés au Bureau des
Objets Trouvés. Parmi ces objets, les documents d'identité suivants:

PC PDIV

Vous disposez d'un délai de 2 mois pour les retirer, en vous présentant aux heures indiquées, avec la présente
lettre, et une pièce d'identité (ou la déclaration de perte établie dans un commissariat de police).
Eventuellement, ces objets pourront être remis à toute personne, munie de sa pièce d'identité et d'une lettre
de votre main l'y autorisant.
Un droit de garde d'un montant de 27,00 francs minimum sera perçu sur place au moment du retrait.
Dans le cas où ils ne seraient pas retirés dans le délai prescrit il en sera disposé, conformémént à la
règlementation en vigueur.

Veuillez agréer, Monsieur, l' assurance de ma considération distinguée.

Le Service des Objets Trouvés,

Légende explicative des codes des objets trouvés ayant une identité

‡ CB	Cartes Bancaires	‡ PC	Permis de Conduire
‡ CHQ	Chéquier	‡ CFN	Carte Famille Nombreuse
‡ LCE	Livret C.E.	‡ PAS	Passeport
‡ VAL	Valeur (50F et +)	‡CSS	Carte Sécurité Sociale
‡ SOM	Somme de - 50F	‡ CO	Carte Orange
‡ CNI	Carte d'identité	‡ PDIV	Papiers Divers
‡ TS	Titre de Séjour		

NOTA : L'Administration ne peut se charger de l'envoi des objets.

Translation of Notice of Property Found

DIRECTION DE LA CIRCULATION
DES TRANSPORTS ET DU COMMERCE   Ref. O.T.:012089

4ème Bureau - Lost Property   PARIS: 21/11/1998
36 rue des Morillons
75732 PARIS CEDEX 15

Tél: 01 45 31 98 11

Open all day Monday and Wednesday 8.30 - 17.00 Tuesday and Thursday 8.30 - 20.00
Friday 8.30 - 17.30 July and August 8.30 - 17.00 Métro CONVENTION Buses 89, PC, 62

MR: ALLEN Richard
XXXXXX   XX
YYYYY
Great Britain

Dear Sir,

I have to inform you that items or documents bearing your name and address have been handed in at the
Lost Property Office. Amongst these items, the following identity documents:

PC PDIV

You have two months to claim them in person between the stated times, by presenting this letter and proof
of identity (or a Statement of Loss made in a Police Station).
If wished, these items may be handed over to anyone with proof of identity and a letter of authority from
you.
An administrative fee of a minimum 27.00 FF will be charged for their release.
In the event of non-withdrawal within the time limit , they will be disposed of according to the regulations
currently in force.

Yours faithfully,

Lost Property Office,

Legend: (Only items relevant to UK citizens are translated)

‡ CB	Bank Cards	‡ PC	Driving Licence
‡ CHQ	Cheque Book	‡ CFN	Carte Famille Nombreuse
‡ LCE	Livret C.E.	‡ PAS	Passport
‡ VAL	Valeur (50F et +)	‡CSS	Carte Sécurité Sociale
‡ SOM	Sum of - 50F	‡ CO	Carte Orange
‡ CNI	ID Card	‡ PDIV	Assorted documents
‡ TS	Residence Permit		

NOTE: the Office cannot forward items

6

Health check

First aid and medical advice (small fee) are available from chemists: (**pharmacie** - green cross sign). There is often a night bell for use in emergencies e.g. obtaining very urgent prescriptions - but do check that the

chemist is on call before waking her / him up! Rotas showing the **Pharmacie de Garde** and the **Médecin de Garde** (Duty Chemist and Doctor) are displayed in the chemists' windows and published in newspapers. The local **Gendarmerie** will also have details of emergency medical arrangements. It is advisable to take out comprehensive insurance cover as the recipient of medical treatment in French hospitals or clinics must pay the bill. British citizens should also fill in Form E111 at any Post Office. This entitles the holder to urgent treatment for accident or unexpected illness in EU countries. A refund of part of the costs of treatment can be obtained in person or by post on application to the local Social Security Office (CPAM). It is as well to remember that certain medical practices are different on the Continent: for example, do not put the thermometer in your mouth! Doctors often prescribe suppositories where in the UK, oral preparations would be used; eg for headaches. Many medicines are also in ampoules and a file is provided for making a nick on the neck prior to snapping the end and pouring the contents into a glass. Make sure you read the instructions carefully. Off-the-shelf remedies tend not to be sold in supermarkets. The "**Droguerie**" is an ironmongers!

Ambulances

Ambulances are privately owned and run, often by a small local firm. As such they have to be paid for by the patient. In some large cities such as Paris, dialling 15 will fetch the **SAMU**, an emergency ambulance service. Sometimes the **Sapeurs-Pompiers** (Fire and Rescue Service) will turn out if other services are not available. They are fully equipped as paramedics to deal with casualties - even pregnancies!

Private ambulances are often to be seen lurking at notorious accident blackspots during busy weekends in order to beat the opposition to a job. Trade can be busy!

Doctors, dentists and prescriptions

It is essential to check before obtaining treatment that the practitioner is working within the state system; that s/he is conventionné(e). After treatment the doctor or dentist should give you a signed certificate of treatment, the **Feuille de Soins**. This is necessary for claiming a refund.

You will have to pay for the consultation and treatment. The amount should be shown on the **Feuille de Soins**. Medicines must also be paid for at the chemist's. The prescription (**ordonnance**) will be given back by the pharmacist. The medicine containers themselves carry detachable labels (**vignettes**) showing the cost and name of the drugs. These are to be removed and stuck to the **Feuille de Soins** which is then signed and dated. The refund application consisting of the Form E111, **Feuille de Soins** and the **Ordonnance** is then taken or sent to the local **CPAM**. Refunds will be sent to your home address after itemised notification of the amount due. It can take some weeks.

Approximately 70% of medical fees and between 35% and 65% of most prescribed medicines is refunded. The cost of some cheaper items is refunded at the lower rate. The blue **Vignettes** are refunded at 40%, the white at 70%. Unrefundable costs are marked with a small triangle on the vignette. It is sensible to make a photocopy of your claim before handing over or posting it. It is also a good move to keep spare copies of the E111 for use in further emergencies.

Specialists may be easily consulted on payment without a referral. GP's tend to display their particular interests on their brass plaques.

Refunds and information

Paris:

Caisse Primaire d'Assurance Maladie, Service des Relations Internationales, 173-175 Rue de Bercy, 75586 Paris Cédex 12. :   01 43 46 12 53

Provinces:

Local **CPAM's** are situated in towns.

Note: Many travellers have experienced difficulties in using an E 111 if issued in a year prior to that of the claim. It used to be the case that an annual form was needed, but this was years ago! The French authorities do not seem to have realized that clause 3.2 now provides for cover for an indefinite period from the date entered on the form! Argue! It is an EU legal right.

Hospital treatment

Outpatient treatment must be paid for in full and a refund claimed as above.

For in-patient treatment, the doctor you have consulted or the hospital doctor will provide a certificate **(attestation).** The hospital should then send a Notice of Admission-Acceptance of Responsibility (**Avis d'admission - prise en charge**) together with your E111 to the **CPAM**. If not, you must do this yourself. 75% of the cost of treatment in hospital is settled by the **CPAM** and the balance must be paid direct by you to the hospital. There will probably also be a fixed daily charge (the **Tarif Journalier**) for non-medical facilities such as food. The 25% and the **Tarif Journalier** are non-refundable, hence the need for separate UK travel insurance.

Medical

- Dentist
- Doctor
- Optician
- Pharmacist
- Hospital

Accident and Emergency Unit	(Service des) Urgences ms
after meals	après les repas
ampoule / blister	ampoule fs
angina	angine fs
antiseptic ointment	onguent antiseptique ms
appendicitis	appendicite fs
appointment to see Dr ...	avec le Docteur ...
are you vaccinated against tetanus?	êtes-vous vacciné(e) contre le tétanos?
are you within the state system?	vous êtes conventionné?
a.s.a.p.	dès que possible
asthma	asthme ms
at the back	au fond
at the bottom	en bas
at the dentist's	chez le dentiste
at the front	devant
at the top	en haut
blood sample	prélèvement de sang ms

blood sugar level	taux de sucre dans le sang ms
boil	furoncle ms
booster innoculation, vaccination	rappel ms
breathe in	respirez / inspirez
breathe out	soufflez / expirez
bruise	bleu ms / contusion fs
bruises on the arms / legs	des contusions au bras / jambes
can I have an appointment ... ?	puis-je avoir un rendez-vous ... ?
can I make an (urgent) appointment?	puis-je prendre un rendez-vous (urgent) ?
can I see a doctor?	puis-je voir un médecin?
can you call a doctor for me?	pouvez-vous m'appeler un médecin?
can you change the lenses?	pouvez-vous changer les verres?
can you do a temporary job?	pouvez-vous faire un traitement provisoire?
can you do it at once?	vous pouvez le faire tout de suite?
can you give me a prescription?	pouvez-vous me donner une ordonnance?
can you give me a signed treatment sheet?	pouvez-vous me donner une feuille de soins?
can you give me / recommend something for ... ?	vous pouvez me donner / conseiller quelque chose pour ... ?
can you hear me?	vous pouvez m'entendre?
can you let me have another?	pouvez-vous m'en donner un(e) autre?
can you numb it?	pouvez-vous faire une anesthésie locale?
can you prescribe me some ... ?	vous pouvez me faire une ordonnance pour ... ?
can you put it back for me?	pouvez-vous me la remettre?
can you recommend a good dentist?	pouvez-vous m'indiquer un bon dentiste?
can you recommend a ... ?	pouvez-vous m'indiquer un / une ... ?
can you recommend one?	pouvez-vous m'en recommander un?
can you recommend something for ... ?	pouvez-vous me conseiller quelque chose pour ... ?
can you repair them for me?	pouvez-vous me les réparer?
can you repair this denture?	pouvez-vous réparer ce dentier?
can you straighten the frame please?	pouvez-vous défausser la monture svp?
chill	refroidissement ms
cold	rhume ms
come back in three days	revenez me voir dans trois jours
concussion	commotion cérébrale fs
cough mixture	antitussif ms / sirop pour la toux ms
cough sweets	pastilles pour la toux fpl
could the doctor come and see me?	le médecin, pourrait-il venir me voir?
could you have a look at it?	pourriez-vous l'examiner?
could you write me another prescription?	pourriez-vous m'établir une nouvelle ordonnance?
couldn't you possibly make it sooner?	ne pourriez-vous pas me prendre plus tôt?
course of treatment	traitement ms
cramp	crampe fs

dentist	chirurgien-dentiste ms
detachable label (on medicines)	vignette fs
diarrhoea	diarrhée fs
dislocate one's shoulder	se déboîter / se démettre l'épaule
dislocate one's wrist	se luxer le poignet
do I have to call back?	je dois repasser?
do I have to go into hospital?	sera-t-il nécessaire de m'hospitaliser?
do I have to have an operation?	je dois me faire opérer?
do I need an operation?	faudra-t-il m'opérer?
do you sell contact lense solution?	vendez vous un liquide pour les verres de contact?
do you sell disposable razors?	vendez-vous les rasoirs jetables?
do you sell homeopathic medicines?	vendez-vous les médicaments homéopathiques?
does it hurt (when you move)?	cela vous fait mal (quand vous bougez)?
does it hurt here?	avez-vous mal là?
does my husband / wife know?	mon mari / ma femme est au courant?
does that hurt?	est-ce que cela vous fait mal?
dose	posologie fs
dull / throbbing / continual / sharp / intermittent	sourde / lancinante / persistante / aiguë / intermittente
duty doctor / chemist	médecin / pharmacien de garde ms
eye specialist	oculiste ms
female nurse	infirmière fs
for my health insurance	pour mon assurance-maladie
for tomorrow	pour demain
gargle	gargarisme ms
gastro-enteritis / stomach upset	gastro-enterite fs
get undressed to the waist	déshabillez-vous jusqu'à la ceinture
GP	généraliste ms
gynaecologist	gynécologue ms
have a prescription made up	faire exécuter une ordonnance
have you a crepe bandage?	avez-vous une bande Velpeau?
have you a mirror?	vous avez un miroir?
have you a roll of sticking plaster?	avez-vous du sparadrap?
have you a temperature?	faites-vous de la température?
have you an appointment?	avez-vous pris rendez-vous?
have you any contact lens liquid?	avez-vous un liquide pour verres de contact?
hayfever	rhume des foins ms
he has been bitten by a dog	il a été mordu par un chien
he has been seriously hurt	il a été grièvement blessé
he has burnt himself	il s'est brûlé
he is unconscious	il a perdu connaissance
heart monitor	moniteur cardiaque ms

heart rhythm	rythme du coeur ms
here	ici
here is my E111	voici mon formulaire E111
hospital facilities	service hospitalier ms
how long have you had it?	vous l'avez depuis combien de temps?
how long have you had this pain?	depuis quand avez-vous cette douleur?
how shall I be refunded?	comment serai-je remboursé?
I am allergic to penicillin	je suis allergique à la pénicilline
I am badly sunburnt	j'ai attrapé un mauvais coup de soleil
I am constipated	je suis constipé(e)
I am diabetic	je suis diabétique
I am Doctor ...	je suis le docteur ...
I am giving you a prescription	je vous fais / rédige une ordonnance
I am giving you some tablets	je vais vous donner des cachets
I am going to check your BP	je vais prendre votre tension
I am going to check your pulse	je vais vous tâter le pouls
I am going to examine you	je vais vous examiner
I am going to get a blood test done	je vais vous faire faire une analyse de sang
I am going to sound your chest	je vais vous ausculter
I am going to take a blood sample	je vais vous faire un prélèvement de sang
I am going to take your temperature	je vais prendre votre température
I am going to X-Ray it	je vais vous faire une radiographie
I am ill	je suis malade
I am long / shortsighted	je suis presbyte / myope
I am on the Pill	je prends la pilule
I am perspiring a lot	je transpire beaucoup
I am pregnant	je suis enceinte
I am putting you on a diet	je vais vous mettre au régime
I am shivery / feel sick	j'ai des frissons / nausées
I am sneezing a lot	j'éternue beaucoup
I am taking this medicine	je prends ces médicaments
I banged my head	je me suis cogné la tête
I can't move my ...	je ne peux pas bouger le / la / les ...
I cannot sleep	je n'arrive pas à dormir
I don't feel well	je ne me sens pas bien
I don't know my blood group	je ne sais pas quel est mon groupe sanguin
I don't want an extraction	je ne voudrais pas me la faire arracher
I feel better now	je me sens mieux maintenant
I feel dizzy	j'ai des vertiges / je suis pris de vertiges
I feel hot / cold	j'ai chaud / froid
I feel sick	j'ai mal au coeur
I feel weak	je me sens faible

I feel weak at the knees	mes genoux se dérobent sous moi
I gashed my arm on a nail	je me suis ouvert le bras sur un clou
I had a heart attack ... years ago	j'ai eu une crise cardiaque il y a ... ans
I have a bad cough	j'ai une mauvaise toux
I have a cough	j'ai la toux
I have a furry tongue	j'ai la bouche pâteuse
I have a pain here	j'ai mal là
I have a pain in the chest	je ressens une douleur dans la poitrine
I have a pain there	j'ai une douleur là
I have a rash here	j'ai une éruption là
I have a swollen hand	J'ai la main enflée
I have a temperature of 38 degrees	j'ai 38 de température
I have a very sore throat	j'ai très mal à la gorge
I have a weak heart	j'ai le coeur faible
I have an abcess	j'ai un abcès
I have an appointment with Doctor X at ...	j'ai rendez-vous avec le docteur X à ...
I have backache / kidney pain	j'ai mal aux reins
I have been stung	quelque chose m'a piqué
I have been stung by a wasp / bee	j'ai été piqué(e) par une guêpe / abeille
I have been vomiting	j'ai eu des vomissements
I have broken a tooth	je me suis cassé une dent
I have broken my arm / ankle / leg / wrist	je me suis cassé le bras / la cheville / la jambe / le poignet
I have broken my crown	j'ai cassé ma couronne
I have broken my denture	j'ai cassé mon dentier
I have broken my glasses	j'ai cassé mes lunettes

I have broken the nose pad of my glasses	j'ai cassé la plaquette de mes lunettes
I have burnt my hand / leg / ankle / wrist	je me suis brûlé la main / la jambe / la cheville / le poignet
I have come out in a rash	j'ai une éruption
I have continual nosebleeds	je saigne constamment du nez
I have cramp in my leg	j'ai une crampe à la jambe
I have cut my finger	je me suis coupé au doigt

I have damaged my glasses by sitting on them	j'ai esquinté mes lunettes en m'asseyant dessus
I have diarrhoea	j'ai la diarrhée
I have difficulty in ...	j'ai du mal à ...
I have difficulty in breathing	j'ai de la peine à respirer
I have earache	j'ai mal aux oreilles
I have got a graze	je me suis fait une éraflure
I have had a fall	j'ai fait une chute
I have had it since yesterday	j'ai cela depuis hier
I have hard / soft lenses	j'ai des verres de contact durs / souples
I have high blood pressure	je fais de l'hypertension
I have hurt my ...	je me suis fait mal au / à la ...
I have indigestion	j'ai une indigestion
I have lost a contact lens	j'ai perdu un verre de contact
I have lost a filling	j'ai perdu un plombage
I have lost the little screw which holds on the arm	j'ai perdu la petite vis qui attache la branche
I have no appetite	je n'ai plus d'appétit
I have pulled a muscle	j'ai claqué un muscle
I have scalded my hand / arm / leg	je me suis ébouillanté la main / le bras / la jambe
I have something in my right / left eye	j'ai quelque chose dans l'oeil droit / gauche
I have sprained my ankle / wrist	je me suis fait une entorse à la cheville / au poignet
I have swollen glands	j'ai une inflammation des ganglions
I have to take a blood sample	je dois vous faire une prise de sang
I have tooth ache	j'ai mal aux dents
I have twisted my ankle / wrist	je me suis foulé la cheville / le poignet
I hurt my back trying to lift ...	je me suis fait mal au dos en essayant de soulever ...
I need a doctor	je veux voir un médecin
I need a doctor, quickly	j'ai besoin d'un médecin, vite
I need a specimen	j'ai besoin d'un spécimen
I need a urine sample	il me faut un échantillon d'urine ms
I need an antiseptic	j'ai besoin d'un antiseptique
I need antibiotics	j'ai besoin d'antibiotiques
I need to see a doctor	il faut que je consulte un médecin
I saw stars	j'ai vu trente-six chandelles
I suffer from insomnia	je souffre de l'insomnie
I think I have caught the flu	je crois que j'ai attrapé un rhume
I think I have food poisoning	je crois que j'ai une intoxication alimentaire
I was sick several times (in the night)	j'ai vomi plusieurs fois (cette nuit)
I wonder if you have a little screw?	vous n'auriez pas une petite vis?
I would like some paracetamol	je voudrais du paracétamol
I would like something for travel sickness	je voudrais quelque chose contre le mal des transports

I would like this prescription made up	je voudrais faire exécuter cette ordonnance
I would like to see a woman doctor	je voudrais voir une femme docteur
I'd like a sight test	je voudrais faire contrôler ma vue
I'd like a spectacle case	je voudrais un étui à lunettes
I'd like an appointment with Dr X	je voudrais un rendez-vous avec le Docteur X
I'd like some contact lenses	je voudrais des verres de contact
I'd like tinted lenses	je voudrais des verres teintés
I'd like to buy a pair of sunglasses	je voudrais acheter des lunettes de soleil
I'll give you a painkiller / antiseptic	je vais vous donner un calmant / antiseptique
I'm going to give you a painkilling injection	je vais vous faire une piqûre analgésique
I'm going to give you an injection	je vais vous faire une piqûre
I've got something in the left / right eye	j'ai reçu quelque chose dans l'oeil gauche / droite
indigestion	indigestion fs
infection	infection fs
is Dr X National Health Service?	le Docteur X est conventionné par la Sécurité Sociale?
is there a doctor here?	y a-t-il un médecin ici?
it hurts	cela me fait mal
it hurts (a lot)	ça fait (très) mal
it is an emergency	c'est une urgence
it is bleeding	elle saigne
it is infected	c'est infecté
it is inflamed	c'est enflammé
it is nothing to worry about	ce n'est pas grave / ce n'est rien
it is obtainable only on prescription	c'est délivré / vendu seulement sur ordonnance
it is very painful	c'est très douloureux
itch	démangeaison fs
lie down	allongez-vous
lot / little	très mal / un peu
lung / heart operation	opération au poumon / coeur fs
make up a prescription	exécuter une ordonnance
male nurse	infirmier ms
may I have a receipt?	puis-je avoir une quittance?
medicine	médicament ms
medical treatment	soins médicaux mpl
migraine / severe headache	migraine fs
mouth ulcer	aphte ms
mouthwash	eau dentrifice fs / élixir dentaire ms
must I stay in bed?	dois-je garder le lit?
my ... hurts (a lot)	j'ai (très) mal à la ... / au ... / aux ... / à l'...
my ankle is swollen	ma cheville est enflée
my arm is broken	mon bras est cassé

115

my blood group is ...	mon groupe sanguin est ...
my blood pressure is too low / high	ma tension est trop basse / élevée
my crown has broken	ma couronne s'est cassée
my crown has come unstuck	ma couronne s'est détachée
my denture has broken	mon dentier s'est cassé
my filling has come out	mon plombage est parti / a sauté
my tongue is coated	j'ai la langue chargée
one of my teeth is hurting	j'ai une dent qui me fait mal
open your mouth	ouvrez la bouche
pill	pilule fs
plasters	pansements adhésifs mpl
please give me a certificate of treatment	ayez l'obligeance de me donner une feuille de soins
please follow my finger with your eyes	veuillez suivre mon doigt des yeux
prescription	ordonnance fs
put out your tongue	montrez-moi votre langue
put your tongue out	tirez la langue
results of tests	résultat des analyses ms
roll up your sleeve	retroussez votre manche
send for a doctor	faites venir un médecin
shall I be able to go out	pourrai-je sortir demain?
she has cut her head open	elle s'est fendu le crâne
she has dislocated her shoulder	elle s'est démis l'épaule
she has hurt herself	elle s'est fait mal
should I see a doctor?	faut-il voir un médecin?
sprained / broken / torn / dislocated	foulé / cassé / déchiré / déboîté
sunblock	écran solaire total ms
sunburn	coup de soleil ms
suntan lotion	lotion solaire fs / lait solaire ms
suntan oil	huile solaire fs
suppository	suppositoire ms
swallow	avaler
tablet	cachet ms / comprimé ms
take this prescription to the chemist	allez chez le pharmacien avec cette ordonnance
take this three times per day	prenez ceci trois fois par jour
teaspoon	cuillerée à café fs
the arm has come off	la branche s'est détachée
the frame is bent	la monture est tordue
the frame is broken	la monture est cassée
the gum is swollen	la gencive est enflée
the gum is very painful	la gencive est très douloureuse
there has been an accident	il est arrivé un accident
there is a swelling here	c'est enflé là

there / here	là
this tooth hurts	cette dent me fait mal
to be taken by mouth, orally	à prendre par voie orale
to gargle	gargariser
to the waist	jusqu'à la ceinture
toothpaste	pâte dentifrice fs
transfusion	transfusion fs
ulcer	ulcère ms
ward	salle fs
we are going to operate on your heart	on va vous opérer du coeur
we shall have to make some tests	il va falloir faire des analyses
what are the surgery hours?	quelles sont les heures de consultation?
what is your blood group?	quel est votre groupe sanguin?
what medicine have you been taking?	quels remèdes prenez-vous?
what sort of pain have you?	quel genre de douleur éprouvez-vous?
what time could he come?	à quelle heure pourrait-il venir?
when can you have them ready?	pour quand pouvez-vous me les réparer?
when will I be fit to travel?	quand serai-je en état de voyager?
when will it be ready?	quand sera-t-il prêt?
when will they be ready?	quand seront-elles prêtes?
where can I find a doctor who speaks English?	où puis-je trouver un médecin qui parle anglais?
where does it hurt?	où avez-vous mal? / où est-ce que cela vous fait mal?
where is the surgery?	où est le cabinet de consultation?
will you notify my family / husband / wife?	voulez- vous bien avertir ma famille / mon mari / ma femme?
wound	blessure fs
you are hurting me	vous me faites mal
you have a heart problem	vous êtes cardiaque
you have an abcess	vous avez un abcès
you have appendicitis	vous avez l'appendicite
you have had a heart attack	vous avez eu une crise cardiaque
you have heart trouble	une maladie de coeur
you have high / low blood pressure	vous faites de l'hypertension / hypotension
you must stay in hospital for several days	vous devez faire un séjour de quelques jours
you need a plaster	il faudra vous mettre un plâtre
you need an X Ray	il faut vous faire une radio
you need to visit the hospital	il faut que vous alliez à l'hôpital
you will have to be admitted	vous devez être hospitalisé(e)
your ... is broken	votre ... est cassé(e)
your ... needs to be X-rayed	il faut faire radiographier ...

7

Socializing

Etiquette Tips

Whilst away you may be lucky enough to be invited into a French home, caravan or tent.

- An invitation for apéritifs is just that! Do not stay for more than about an hour.

- **NEVER** use the familiar **"TU"** to adults, however well you may think you know them, **unless invited to do so**. It is an insult (implying social inferiority) to anyone other than close friends, very young children or animals. Cats are also candidates for the **"vous"**!! Younger people do use **"tu"** on first acquaintance, but take your cue from the French person.

- Handshakes (**le shake-hand** in French!) are not the pump-action variety as in the UK! A brief clasp is all that is required. If someone has his / her hands full, for example if carrying something, it is not unusual to be offered an elbow or a finger to grasp!

- Do not arrive early or late. If the latter is unavoidable try to explain.

- Whisky is often appreciated as a gift.

- Do not bring wine - it may well be taken as an insult - an aspersion on the quality of the Host's Cellar!

- Take flowers to your hostess - but be warned - take odd numbers: seven is a good number - **never** 13. Do not under any circumstances give chrysanthemums. One youthful and highly embarrassed Englishman of my acquaintance had them promptly, firmly and not very politely rejected. (They are for funerals and **la Toussaint**  - All Saints!) Carnations are bad luck - probably for the florist who cannot sell them! Red roses are ONLY for lovers and close friends of the opposite sex.

- When offered an **apéritif**, wait to see what is proposed before choosing.

- Wait to be shown to your place if it is that sort of occasion.

- Wait until everyone has been served before starting to eat.

- Let your host(ess) serve the wine - do not help yourself.

- Remember that "**merci**" when you are offered something usually means "no thank you".

- Wait until everyone has been served before drinking.

- If you do not want to drink too much, keep a fairly full glass all the time - emptying it will result in a swift refill from your host(ess).

- Side plates for bread are unusual. It is acceptable to put bread on the table surface.

- Talk about previous memorable meals you have eaten and wines you have drunk - in France of course!

- Discuss the food and wine and be complimentary - say what you enjoy about it.

- Do not smoke during a meal.

- Try to keep a little room for each course - the cheese can be a particularly difficult one after a huge starter, **entrée** and main course.

- Keep some drink back for a toast, if it is that sort of formal occasion.

- Resting one's wrists on the table is allowed - in fact it is considered impolite to put your hands on your knees or in your lap. They are supposed to remain in view! A Gallic precaution perhaps?

- As you leave, shake hands with everyone, thank and compliment the host(ess).

Restaurant / Café / Hotel

- Prices, including service charges, must be displayed outside the establishment.

- Cafés must show the prices of black coffee, draught beer, fruit juice, spring water.

- Restaurants must display "**menus du jour**" as including or not including, drinks. (**Boissons (non) comprises** - Drinks (not) included).

- Cabarets or clubs providing entertainment must indicate whether the entry fee includes a drink and specifying what kind.

- Hotel prices must be displayed in the room as well as in the reception.

- **PRIX NET** is the price inclusive of service.

- Do remember that **it is not permitted to buy a drink at the bar** and then sit at a table as is the custom in the UK. There is an additional charge for sitting and the waiter service.

- You do not pay for your drink at the time of service - the waiter will leave a till receipt which he tears partly in half on payment.

- Do not call the waiter "**Garçon**" but "**Monsieur**", accompanied, if necessary to attract his attention, by raising the index finger. Waitresses are addressed as "**Madame**" or "**Mademoiselle**" as appropriate.

Accommodation, Food and Drink

- **Bar**
- **Café**
- **Hotel**
- **Restaurant**

(fish) ... doesn't agree with me	je ne supporte pas ... (le poisson)
add to the bill	ajouter à la note
almost raw (meat)	bleue (viande)
and a kir / a (bottled) beer	et comme boisson, un kir / une bière
and for vegetables?	et comme légumes?
another blanket	autre couverture fs
another glass	autre verre ms
another pillow	autre oreiller ms
are meals included in the price?	les repas sont-ils inclus dans le prix?
as a paying guest	en hôte payant
bill	note fs
breakfast is served from ...	le petit déjeuner est servi à partir de ...
by return post	par retour du courrier
call me at ...	réveillez-moi à ...
can I have a quiet room?	puis-je avoir une chambre calme?
can I have an early breakfast?	puis-je prendre le petit déjeuner de bonne heure?
can I have an early call tomorrow?	pouvez-vous me réveiller demain de bonne heure?
can I see the room?	puis-je voir la chambre?

can I telephone from here?	puis-je téléphoner d'ici?
can we have breakfast in our room?	pouvons-nous prendre le petit déjeuner dans notre chambre?
can you call me a taxi please?	pouvez-vous m'appeler un taxi svp?
can you make up my bill please?	pouvez-vous préparer ma note svp?
carafe of house wine	pichet du réserve du patron ms
clean towel	serviette propre fs
coathanger	cintre ms
could we have an ashtray?	pourriez-vous nous apporter un cendrier?
could you bring me ... ?	pourriez-vous m'apporter ... ?
could you call a taxi for me please?	pouvez-vous m'appeler un taxi svp?
could you forward my mail?	pouvez-vous faire suivre mon courrier?
could you prepare us ... ?	pourriez-vous nous préparer ... ?
cut to order (cheese etc)	à la coupe (fromage etc)
did you enjoy the meal?	le repas vous a-t-il plu?
dining room	salle de restaurant fs
disgusting	infecte
do you like it?	vous aimez?
do you serve vegetarian?	servez-vous les repas végétariens?
do you take a deposit?	vous faut-il des arrhes?
do you want me to spell it?	voulez-vous que je l'épelle?
does one have to leave the key at reception?	faut-il laisser la clef à la réception?
does the price include full board?	est-ce que le tarif comprend la chambre et tous les repas?
don't you like it?	vous n'aimez pas?
double bedded room	une chambre avec un grand lit
draught beer	une pression
dry cleaning tariff	tarif du nettoyage
Eat As Much As You Like	Buffet à Volonté
emergency exit	sortie de secours fs
for my taste	à mon goût
for one person	pour une personne
for one / two / three nights	pour une / deux / trois nuits
for the nights of 6th and 7th March next	pour les nuits du 6 et 7 mars prochain
for when?	pour quand?
from 15th to 17th September	du 15 au 17 septembre
Free Tasting	Dégustation
from what time?	à partir de quelle heure?
full board	pension complète fs
give me another pillow	donnez-moi un autre oreiller
give me my ... which is in the safe	donnez-moi mon / ma ... qui est au coffre
half board	demi-pension fs

have cleaned	faire nettoyer
have ironed	faire repasser
have you a double / twin bedded room?	avez-vous une chambre double / à deux lits?
have you a room free?	avez-vous une chambre de libre?
have you a table for one?	avez-vous une table pour une personne?
have you a table further from ... ?	auriez-vous une table plus éloignée de ... ?
have you enough?	vous en avez assez?
have you had sugar?	vous êtes sucré?
help yourself!	servez-vous!
here is my passport	voici mon passeport
I am allergic to seafood	je suis allergique aux fruits de mer
I am leaving tomorrow morning	je vais partir demain matin
I am not very hungry	je n'ai pas tellement faim
I am paying / it's my round	c'est moi qui paye
I am staying until 3rd May	je reste jusqu'au 3 mai
I am very thirsty	j'ai très soif
I can do nothing / there's no room for tonight	je ne peux rien pour ce soir
I cannot have any ... for a week	je suis interdit de ... pour une semaine
I can't stand ...	j'ai horreur de ...
I can't stand noise	je ne supporte pas le bruit
I don't like ... very much	je n'aime pas trop ...
I don't really fancy ...	je n'ai pas trop / tellement envie de ...
I hate …	je déteste …
I have no identity card	je n'ai pas de carte d'identité
I have only ...	il ne me reste que ...
I have to cancel	je dois annuler
I haven't any ...	il ne me reste pas de ...
I insist	j'insiste
I like meat	j'aime bien la viande
I ordered it well done	j'ai demandé du bien cuit
I phoned this morning to book a table	j'ai téléphoné ce matin pour réserver une table
I prefer fish to meat	je préfère le poisson à la viande
I want to stay 3 nights	je veux rester trois nuits
I was held up at the airport	j'ai été retenu à l'aéroport
I'll have ... instead	je prends plutôt ...
ice	glaçon ms
I'd like some flowers on the table	je voudrais des fleurs sur la table
I'd like to book a room	je voudrais réserver une chambre
I'd like to know	je voudrais savoir
I'd like to pay by credit card	je voudrais payer par carte de crédit
I'd like to pay cash	je voudrais payer en liquide
I'd like to see the chef	je voudrais voir le chef de cuisine

I'd like to see the menu	je voudrais voir la carte du jour
I'd like to see the owner	je voudrais voir le patron
I'll buy you an apéritif	je vous paie un apéro
I'll have ...	pour moi ...
I'll send you a deposit	je vous envoie des arrhes
I'll take it	je le / la prends
I'm mad about seafood	je raffole des fruits de mer
I'm not very fond of meat	je ne suis pas très viande
I'm very annoyed	je suis vraiment contrarié
in bed and breakfast	en chambre d'hôte
in private	en tête à tête
in the area	dans les environs
in the name of ...	au nom de ...
in the shade / on the terrace / with a view of ...	à l'ombre / en terrasse / avec une vue sur ...
in what name?	c'est à quel nom?
is it easy to park?	peut-on se garer sans difficulté?
is the cover charge included?	le couvert est-il compris?
is the voltage 220?	est-ce que le courant est à 220 volts?
is there a group playing	y a-t-il un groupe qui joue ici le soir?
is there a message for me?	y a-t-il un message pour moi?
is there a night porter?	y a-t-il un gardien de nuit?
is there a private car park?	y a-t-il un parking privé?
is there satellite TV?	recevez-vous les programmes par satellite?
it is (a little) (too) salty / cooked /sweet	c'est (un peu) (trop) salé / cuit / sucré
it is for a booking	c'est pour une réservation
it is thirst-quenching	ça désaltère
it is very thirst-quenching	c'est très désaltérant
it is white / pink / red	c'est du blanc / rosé / rouge
it tastes funny	ça a un goût bizarre / un drôle de goût
it's booked	c'est noté
it's just what I need	c'est juste ce qu'il me faut
just what the doctor ordered	la petite goutte du médecin
laundry service	service de blanchisserie ms
leave it then!	laissez donc!
liqueur	digestif / pousse-café ms
lobster does not agree with me	le homard ne me réussit pas
looking onto ...	donnant sur ...
more gravy / sauce please	encore de la sauce svp
milk (full cream / skimmed / semi - skimmed)	lait ms (entier / écrémé / demi - écrémé)
overlooking the courtyard	côté cour
overlooking the street	côté rue
overnight accommodation	soirée étape

per night	par nuitée
per person	par personne
pillow	oreiller ms
please fill in the slip	veuillez remplir la fiche
Please Report to Reception	Prière de s'Adresser à la Réception
can you have it reheated for me?	pouvez-vous me le / la faire réchauffer?
Press Bell	Appuyer sur le Bouton Sonnerie
rare / medium / well done / very well done	saignant / à point / bien cuit / très bien cuit
room has been booked for me	on a réservé une chambre pour moi
room in a guest house	chambre en pension fs
room service menu	menu servi dans les chambres ms
room with twin beds	une chambre avec lits jumeaux
safe for valuables	un coffre pour les objets de valeur
sauna	sauna ms

shall we drink to that?	on l'arrose?
since there is no alternative	puisqu'il n'y a pas d'autre solution
small portion	petite portion fs
soap	du savon
something not too dear	quelque chose de pas trop cher
something special	quelque chose de spécial
Take Away Food	Vente / Plats à Emporter
taste it	goûtez-voir
that's alright (feasible)	c'est possible
that's right	c'est cela
the lady will have ...	pour madame ...
the ... franc menu	le menu à ... francs
the bill please	l'addition svp

125

the booking is from midday to midday	la location est de midi à midi
the key is in the door	la clé est sur la porte
the lady will have a Spanish omelette	pour madame, une omelette espagnole
the lights are not working	la lumière ne marche pas
the price is per person or per room?	le prix est-il par personne ou par chambre?
there are two of us	nous sommes deux
there is a slug / worm in my salad	il y a une limace / un ver dans ma salade
this ... is cold	ce / cette ... est froid(e)
this is not what I ordered	ce plat n'est pas ce que j'ai commandé
this meat is not cooked enough	cette viande n'est pas assez cuite
this wine is not at room temperature	ce vin n'est pas chambré
this wine is not cool enough	ce vin n'est pas suffisamment frais
two places	deux couverts
valet / dry cleaning service	service de pressing ms
very much	énormément
waiter!	monsieur!
we are a spoon short	il nous manque une cuiller
we haven't decided yet	nous n'avons pas encore choisi
we want adjoining rooms	nous voulons des chambres attenantes
we'll change your room	nous vous changerons de chambre
what are the mealtimes?	quelles sont les heures des repas?
what are your terms?	quels sont vos tarifs et conditions?
what do you recommend?	qu'est-ce que recommandez?
what facilities has the hotel?	quelles prestations l'hôtel a-t-il?
what floor is my room on?	à quel étage est ma chambre?
what is it exactly?	qu'est-ce que c'est au juste?
what is the dish of the day?	quel est le plat du jour?
what is the price of the room?	quel est le prix de la chambre?
what is the voltage here?	le voltage est de combien ici?
what is there to see?	quelles attractions y a-t-il?
what time do you close?	vous fermez à quelle heure?
what time is ... ?	à quelle heure est le ... ?
what will you have to drink?	et comme boisson?
what will you have?	qu'est-ce que vous prenez?
what wine would you recommend?	qu'est-ce que vous recommandez comme vin?
when do you start serving breakfast?	vous servez le petit déjeuner à partir de quelle heure?
when does the hotel close?	à quelle heure l'hôtel ferme-t-il?
where can I deposit my valuables?	où puis-je déposer mes objets de valeur?
where can I leave my luggage?	où puis-je laisser mes bagages?
where can I post a letter?	où puis-je poster une lettre?
will you have another?	vous en voulez un autre?

Wine by the Glass	Vin au Verre
Wine List	Carte des Vins
with a double bed	avec un grand lit
with a family	en famille
with bathroom	avec salle de bain
with shower	avec douche
would it be possible to have ... ?	serait-il possible d'avoir ... ?
would you get my bill ready?	voulez-vous bien préparer ma note?
would you like some more?	vous en reprenez?
you are in room 37	vous êtes au trente-sept
You Can Bring Your Own Food (in a bar)	On Peut Apporter Son Manger
you have made a mistake in the bill	vous vous êtes trompé dans l'addition
you will have an apéritif?	vous prendrez bien un apéritif?

Menus

- Depending on the type of establishment, various options may be offered.

- In tourist areas, the **Menu Touristique** should in general be avoided as it is invariably overpriced and of a poor standard.

- The **Plat du Jour** can be good value as it has fewer pretensions. Three courses and wine are frequently included.

- A frequent excuse for exorbitant prices is the **Menu Gastronomique**, again commonly found in tourist areas noted for their local specialities.

- Menus such as that on the next page permit a choice of one item from each course if there is a **Prix Fixe** or Set Price, otherwise it is acceptable to choose, say, just fish and a dessert.

- The best guide to quality and value for money is the presence of local customers.

- Although it may not be fashionable to say so, it is **not** unusual to be unfortunate enough to eat food in France which is very badly cooked, prepared and served. The wine can even be watered!

- Remember that "rare" when applied to meat in France means just "badly injured"! It is almost impossible to get well done steak.

La Vendange

Carte du Jour

Entrées Froides

Terrine Spéciale
Plateau de fruits de Mer
Moules Farcies

Entrées Chaudes

Escargots de Bourgogne

Poissons

Saumon frais grillé sauce béarnaise
Sole meunière

Viandes

Escalope de veau
Filet au poivre
Filet de boeuf rôti
Bifteck grillé

Légumes

Pommes allumettes
Petits pois à l'étuvée
Céléri au gratin

Fromages

Bleu d'Auvergne
Cantal
Tomme de Savoie
Chèvre
Camembert

Desserts

Crème caramel
Tarte du jour
Profiteroles au chocolat

Service non compris 20%

Menu French

This is rather specialized and subject to regional variations, so the following should be of use in deciphering the choice in most parts of the country

Abricots	Apricots
Agneau	Lamb
Agneau pré-salé	Lamb from salt marshes
Aiglefin	Haddock
Aiguillette	Sliver (Duck breast etc)
Ail	Garlic
Aile	Wing
Aioli	Garlic mayonnaise
Airelles	Wild cranberries
Algue	Edible seaweed
Alose	Shad
Aloyau	Sirloin of beef
Alsacienne, à l'	With sauerkraut, ham and sausages
Amuse-gueule	Appetizer served with apéritif
Amandes	Almonds
Ananas	Pineapple
Anchois	Anchovy
Andouillette	Chitterling sausage
Aneth	Dill
anglaise, à l'	Plain boiled
Anguilles au vert	Eels with white wine and herbs
Anis	Aniseed
Araignée de mer	Spider crab
Armoricaine à l'	Sauce of herbs, tomatoes, white wine, brandy
Artichauts	Artichokes
Asperges	Asparagus
Avelines	Hazelnuts
Avocets	Avocados

Ballotine	Stuffed, boned, rolled poultry
Baie	Berries
Bar (or Loup)	Sea bass
Barbeau	Barbel (river fish)
Barbue	Brill
Basilic	Basil
Basquaise	Basque style: Bayonne ham, rice and red or green peppers
Baudroie	Monkfish
Bavarois	Custard cream dessert, often with fruit
Bavette	Skirt steak
Béarnaise	Sauce flavoured with tarragon and vinegar
Bécasse	Woodcock
Béchamel	White sauce
Beignet	Fritter
Bercy	Sauce based on fish stock or bonemarrow, wine and shallots
Berrichonne (à la)	With bacon, cabbage, onions and chestnuts
Betterave	Beetroot
Beurre blanc	Butter, shallots, wine and vinegar
Beurre noir	Browned butter, vinegar and parsley
Biche	Doe
Bigarade	Bitter orange sauce
Bigorneaux	Winkles
Bisque	Creamy shellfish soup
Blanc (de volaille)	White breast (of poultry)
Blanchaille	Whitebait
Blanquette	Thickened white stew
Bordelais(e)	Sauce of red wine and bone marrow
Bouchée	Tiny filled puff pastry
Boudin	Blood sausage
Boudin blanc	White sausage of veal, chicken or pork
Bouillabaisse	Provençal fish soup
boulangère (à la)	Braised or baked with onions and potatoes
Bourgeoise (à la)	With carrots, onions and bacon
Bouquet	Shrimps
Bourdelot	Fruit (apple or pear) wrapped in pastry
Bourguignonne	Burgundy style; red wine, onions and bacon
Bourride	White fish and shellfish soup with aioli
Brandade de morue	Creamed salt cod with oil and garlic
Brème	Freshwater bream

Bretonne (à la)	Served with haricot beans
Brocciu	Corsican sheep's milk cheese
Brochet	Pike
Brochette	Skewered meat or fish
Brugnons	Nectarines
Bulots	Whelks
Cabillaud	Cod
Cabri	Kid
Caen (à la mode de)	Cooked in Calvados, white wine or cider
Cagouille	Small land snail
Caille	Quail
Calmar	Small squid
Canard	Duck
Cane	Female duck
Caneton	Duckling
Cannelle	Cinnamon
Carbonade de boeuf	Beef braised in beer
Cardinal	Rich red fish sauce with mushrooms, truffles (usually for lobster)
Cargolade	Snails cooked in wine
Carré (d'agneau, de veau)	Rack (of lamb, of veal)
Carrelet	Plaice
Cassis	Black currant, black currant liqueur

Cassoulet	Casserole of white beans with pork, goose or duck and sausages
Céleri	Celery
Céleri-rave	Celeriac
Cèpes	Boletus mushrooms
Cerfeuil	Chervil
Cerises	Cherries
Cerneaux	Green walnuts
Cervelas	Garlic-flavoured cured pork sausage
Cervelles	Brains, of calf or lamb
Champignons	Mushrooms
- sauvages	- wild
- des bois	- woodland
- de Paris	- cultivated
Chanterelles	Chanterelle mushrooms
Chantilly	Sweetened whipped cream
Chapon	Capon
Charcuterie	Cold cuts, smoked, cured or salted meats, terrines, pâtés
Chateaubriand	Thick centre cut of fillet of beef
Charlotte	Moulded dessert with sponge fingers and creamy filling, or fruit purée
Charolais	Noted cattle breed; beef
Chasseur	"Hunter style": White wine, mushroom, tomato and shallot sauce
Châtaigne	Chestnut
Chausson	Pastry turnover
Chemise (en)	Wrapped, generally in pastry
Chèvre	Goat or goat cheese
Chevreuil	Venison
Chicorée	Curly endive or chicory
Chipiron	Basque name for small squid
Choron	Béarnaise sauce with tomato purée
Chou	Cabbage
Choucroute	Sauerkraut; garnie with meat
Chou-fleur	Cauliflower
Ciboules	Spring onions
Ciboulettes	Chives
Citron	Lemon
Citron pressé	Fresh lemon juice
Citron vert	Lime

Citronnelle	Lemon grass
Citrouille	Pumpkin
Civet	Rich stew
Civet de lièvre	Jugged hare
Civettes	Chives
Clafoutis	Batter cake with fruit
Clémentine	Small tangerine
Cochons	Pigs
Cochonnailles	Pork products
Cocotte	Small cooking dish
Coing	Quince
Colin	Hake
Colvert	Wild duck
Compote	Stewed fruit or vegetables
Concombre	Cucumber
Confit	Preserved or candied
Confit de canard (d'oie)	Potted duck (goose) cooked and preserved in its own fat
Confiture	Jam
Congre	Conger eel
Contrefilet	Part of a sirloin
Coque	Cockle
Coquillages	Shellfish
Coquille Saint-Jacques	Sea scallop
Corbeille de fruits	Basket of fresh fruit
Cornichon	Gherkin
Côtelette	Chop
Cou (d'oie)	Neck (of goose)
Coulibiac	Fish cake (usually salmon) in pastry
Coulis	Purée of raw or cooked vegetables or fruit
Courgette	Baby marrow
Court-bouillon	Aromatic poaching liquid
Crabe	Crab
Crécy (à la)	With carrots
Crème anglaise	Custard
Crémet	Fresh cream cheese eaten with sugar & cream
Crêpe	Pancake
Crépinette	Faggot
Cresson	Watercress
Crevettes grises	Shrimps
Crevettes roses	Prawns

Croque-monsieur	Toasted ham and cheese sandwich
Croustade	Mould or puff pastry shell with savoury fillings
Crottin	Firm round goat's cheese
Croûte (en)	Pastry case (in a)
Cru	Raw
Crudité	Raw vegetables
Crustacés	Shellfish
Cuissot	Haunch, of veal, venison or boar
Darne	Slice or steak of fish
Daube	Meat slowly braised in wine and herbs
Daurade	Sea bream
Demi-sel	Lightly salted
Désossé	Boned
Diable	Highly seasoned sauce; also type of cooking pot
Dijonnais (à la)	With mustard sauce
Dinde	Turkey
Dindonneau	Young turkey
Dodine	Cold, boned, stuffed duck
Douceurs	Sweets
Doux, douce	Sweet

Duxelles	Stuffing or seasoning of cooked minced mushrooms
Echalote	Shallot
Ecrevisses	Freshwater crayfish
Emincé	Thin slice
Encornet	Small squid
Endive	Chicory
Entrecôte	Rib steak
Entremets	Desserts
Epaule	Shoulder
Epinards	Spinach
Epis de maïs	Sweetcorn
Escalope	Thin slice
Escargots	Snails
Espadon	Swordfish
Estouffade	As Daube; meat first marinated and browned
Estragon	Tarragon
Etrille	Small crab
Etuvé(e)	Braised
Faisan(e)	Pheasant
Farci(e)	Stuffed
Farine	Flour
Faux-filet	Sirloin steak
Fenouil	Fennel
Feuille de chêne	Oak-leaf lettuce
Feuilletage (en)	In puff pastry
Fève	Broad bean
Fine de claire	Fattened oyster
Flageolets	Kidney beans; fresh green, dried white
Flambé(e)	Flamed
Flan	Sweet or savoury custard
Flétan	Halibut
Foie	Liver
Fond d'artichauts	Artichoke hearts
Forestière (à la)	With mushrooms and bacon
Four (au)	Baked
Fourré(e)	Stuffed or filled
Frais, fraîche	Fresh or chilled
Fraise (des bois)	(Wild) strawberry
Framboise	Raspberry

Frappé	Iced or chilled
Friandise	A sweet
Fricadelles	Small balls of minced meat
Fricandeau	Topside of veal
Fricassé	Stewed or sautéed; braised in wine with cream
Frisée	Curly endive
Frites	French fries / chips
Friture	Small fried fish
Froid(e)	Cold
Fromage	Cheese
Fromage de tête	Pork brawn
Fruits de mer	Seafood
Fumé(e)	Smoked
Fumet	Fish or vegetable stock
Galantine	Cold pressed poultry, meat or fish in jelly
Galette	Pancake or cake, sweet or savoury
Gamba	Large prawn
Garbure	Thick vegetable soup
Gardons	Small roach
Garni	With vegetables
Gâteau	Cake or mould
Gaufre	Waffle
Gelée	Aspic
Genièvre	Juniper berry
Gésier	Gizzard
Gibelotte	Rabbit stewed in wine
Gibier	Game
Gigot	Leg of lamb
Gigue	Haunch
Gingembre	Ginger
Girolle	Wild mushroom
Glacé(e)	Iced or glazed
Glace	Ice cream
Gougère	Cheese enriched choux pastry
Goujon	Gudgeon
Goujonnette	Small fried fillets
Gourmandise	A sweet
Graisse	Fat
Grand veneur	Sauce for game with wine, redcurrants and pepper

Granité	Grainy water ice
Gras double	Tripe in wine with onions
Gratin	Browned topping, often with breadcrumbs or cheese
Gratin dauphinois	Potatoes baked with cream and cheese
Grecque (à la)	Vegetables marinated and cooked in wine, spices and herbs
Grenade	Pomegranate
Grenadin	Small veal scallop
Grenouille (cuisse de)	Frog's leg
Grillade	Grilled meat
Grillé(e)	Grilled
Griotte	Morello cherry
Grive	Thrush
Gros sel	Coarse salt
Groseille, groseille à maquereau	Gooseberry
Groseille rouge	Redcurrant
Groseille noire	Blackcurrant
Hachis	Minced meat or fish
Haddock	Smoked haddock, finnan haddie
Hareng	Herring
Hareng fumé	Kipper
Hareng salé	Bloater
Haricots blancs	Dried white beans
Haricots rouges	Red kidney beans
Haricots verts	French beans
Hochepot	Thick casserole
Hollandaise	Sauce with butter, egg yolk and lemon juice
Homard	Lobster
Huile	Oil
Huître	Oyster
Ile flottante	Floating island
Infusion	Herb tea
Jambon	Ham
Jambon Bayonne / à la bayonnaise	Mild ham cooked partly in wine
Jambon cru	Salt or smoke-cured raw ham
Jambon persillé	Cold ham and parsley in white wine jelly
Jambonneau	Small ham, knuckle of pork
Jardinière	With diced mixed vegetables
Jarret de veau	Veal shin
Julienne	With vegetable matchsticks

Jus	Juice
Lait	Milk
Laitance	Roe
Laitue	Lettuce
Lamproie	Lamprey, eel-like fish
Langouste	Spiny lobster, crayfish
Langoustine	Dublin Bay prawns, scampi
Langue	Tongue
Lapereau	Young rabbit
Lapin	Rabbit
Lard	Bacon
Lardon	Cube of bacon
Laveret	Trout-like lake fish
Léger(ère)	Light
Légume	Vegetable
Lieu	Small salt-water fish
Lièvre	Hare
Limande	Lemon sole
Lisette	Small mackerel
Lotte de mer	Monkfish
Lotte de rivière	Burbot, river fish
Loup (de mer)	Sea-bass
Lyonnaise (à la)	With onions
Macédoine	Diced mixed fruit or vegetables
Mâche	Lamb's lettuce
Madère	Madeira
Magret	Breast (of duck or goose)
Maïs	Sweet corn
Mandarine	Tangerine
Mange-tout	Young peas in the pod, eaten whole
Mangue	Mango
Maquereau	Mackerel
Marbrade	Pig's head in aspic
Marcassin	Young wild boar
Marchand de vin	In a red wine sauce
Marengo (poulet)	Fried chicken, eggs and tomatoes with garlic, brandy and crayfish
Mariné(e)	Marinated
Marjolaine	Marjoram
Marmite	Tall cooking pot
Marquise	Mousse-like chocolate cake

Marron	Large chestnut
Marron glacé	Candied chestnut
Matelote	Freshwater fish stew
Menthe	Mint
Merguez	Spicy sausage
Merlan	Whiting (hake in S.France)
Merle	Blackbird
Mérou	Grouper
Mesclun	Mixture of salad leaves
Meunière (à la)	Fish fried in butter, served with lemon and parsley
Meurette	In or with a red wine sauce
Miel	Honey
Mijoté(e)	Simmered
Millefeuille	Puff pastry with many thin layers
Mirabelle	Small yellow plum
Moelle	Beef marrow
Montmorency	With cherries
Morille	Type of mushroom
Mornay	Cheese sauce
Morue	Salt cod
Mouclade	Mussels in creamy sauce
Moule	Mussel

Moules (à la) marinière	Mussels cooked in white wine with shallots
Mousseline	Hollandaise sauce with whipped cream
Mousseron	Wild mushroom
Moutarde	Mustard
Mouton	Mutton
Mulet	Mullet
Mûres	Blackberries / mulberries
Muscade	Nutmeg
Museau de boeuf	Beef muzzle, usually in a vinaigrette sauce
Myrtilles	Bilberries / blueberries
Nage (à la)	Shellfish poached in court bouillon with herbs
Nantua	Rich truffle and crayfish sauce
Navarin	Lamb stew
Navets	Turnips
Niçoise (Salade)	Type of mixed salad (tuna, egg etc)
Noisette	Small round steak
Noisettes	Hazelnuts
Noix	Nuts, walnuts
Noix (de veau)	Topside of leg (of veal)
Normande (à la)	Normandy style: with mushrooms, eggs and cream or with apple cider and / or Calvados
Nouilles	Noodle
Oeuf à la coque	Soft-boiled egg
Oeuf brouillé	Scrambled egg
Oeuf dur	Hard-boiled egg
Oeuf poché	Poached egg
Oeuf sur le plat	Fried egg
Oeufs à la neige	Floating island
Oie	Goose
Oignon	Onion
Omble chevalier	Freshwater char, type of salmon
Ombre	Grayling
Omelette Norvégienne	Meringue-covered sponge and ice cream, like baked Alaska
Onglet	Flank of beef
Orange (jus d')	Usually canned or bottled orange juice
Orange pressée	Fresh orange juice
Ortie	Nettle
Os	Bone
Oseille	Sorrel
Oursin	Sea urchin

Paillard	Thick slice of veal or chicken breast
Pain	Bread
Palmier (coeurs de)	Palm hearts
Palombe	Wood or wild pigeon
Palourde	Clam
Palourdes farcies	Cooked stuffed clams
Pamplemousse	Grapefruit
Panaché	Mixed; an assortment or shandy
Panais	Parsnips
Pan bagnat	Large bread roll filled with salad, olive oil, anchovies
Papillote (en)	Baked in grease proof paper or foil
Parfait (de)	Creamy iced mousse
Parfum	Flavour
Parmentier	Dish with potatoes
Pastèque	Watermelon
Pâte	Pastry or dough
Pâte brisée	Shortcrust pastry
Pâtes (fraîches)	Pasta (fresh)
Pâtisseries	Pastries
Paupiette	Thin slice of meat or fish stuffed, rolled and braised

Pavé	Thick slice
Peau	Skin
Pêche	Peach
Perdreau	Young partridge
Perdrix	Partridge
Périgourdine (à la)	With truffles and / or foie gras
Périgueux	Sauce with truffles and madeira
Persil	Parsley
Petit-gris	Land snail
Petite marmite	Individual pot of consommé
Petits-pois	Green peas
Pétoncle	Queen scallop
Piballe	Small eel
Pied de porc	Pig's trotter
Pieds et paquets	Stuffed sheep's tripe and trotters
Pigeonneau	Young pigeon, squab
Pignon	Pine nut
Piment	Hot pepper
Piment doux	Sweet pepper
Pintade	Guinea fowl
Pintadeau	Young guinea fowl
Pipérade	Scrambled eggs with onions, green peppers and tomatoes
Piquant(e)	Sharp or spicy
Pissaladière	Dough-based tart of onions, anchovies and black olives
Pissenlits	Dandelion (leaves)
Pistaches	Pistachio nuts
Pistou	Purée of basil, garlic and olive oil
Pithiviers	Puff pastry filled with almond cream
Pleurotte	Oyster mushroom
Plie	Plaice
Pochouse	Stew of eel and other freshwater fish in white wine
Poêlé(e)	Pan-fried
Poire	Pear
Poireau	Leek
Poisson	Fish
Poitrine	Breast of meat or poultry
Poitrine fumée	Smoked bacon
Poivrade	Peppery sauce served with game

Poivre	Pepper
Poivron	Pimento / sweet pepper
Pommeau	apéritif blended from must of cider and Calvados
Pommes	Apples
Pommes de terre	Potatoes
- à l'anglaise	- boiled
- à la vapeur	- steamed
- allumettes	- matchsticks, fried
- boulangère, rôtie	- roast
- frites	- chips
- lyonnaise	- sautéed with onions
- nature, au naturel	- boiled
- purée de	- mashed
Porc	Pork
Porc (carré de)	Loin of pork
Porcelet	Suckling pig
Porto	Port
Portugaise (à la)	With tomatoes
Potage	Thick soup
Pot-au-chocolat	Chocolate dessert
Pot-au-feu	Boiled beef and vegetables
Potée	Hotpot of pork and cabbage
Poularde	Fatted chicken
Poulet	Chicken
Poulet fermier	Free-range chicken
Poulpe	Octopus
Rutabaga	Swede
Sabayon	French version of zabaglione
Sablé	Shortbread
Safran	Saffron
Saint-Germain	With peas
Saint-Pierre	John Dory (mild sea fish)
Saisons (suivant)	Depending on the season
Salade niçoise	Salad including eggs, green beans, olives, anchovies and sometimes tuna
Salade panachée	Mixed salad
Salade	Lettuce or green salad
Salaison	Salt meat / fish
Salmis	Roast joints of game or poultry in a red wine sauce

Sandre	River perch
Sang	Blood
Sanglier	Wild boar
Saucisse	Fresh sausage (sold uncooked)
Saucisson	Larger sausage (sold cooked)
Sauge	Sage
Saumon (fumé)	(Smoked) salmon
Sauté	Browned in fat
Sauvage	Wild
Scarole	Endive
Seiche	Cuttlefish
Sel	Salt
Selle	Saddle (of meat)
Selon grosseur / grandeur	Priced according to size (eg on menu)
Soissonnaise (à la)	With white haricot beans
Sole	Sole
- à la Dieppoise	- fillets with sauce of mussels, shrimps and white wine
- Dugléré	- with tomatoes, onions, herbs and cream sauce
- Marguéry	- with mussels, shrimps and rich egg sauce
- Véronique	- poached in white wine with grapes
Sorbet	Water ice
Soubise	With purée of onions and sometimes rice
Sucre	Sugar
Suprême	Boneless breast of poultry
Tapenade	Purée of black olives, anchovies, capers
Tartare (steak)	Finely minced steak served raw with raw egg yolk, onion and capers
Tarte Tatin	Caramelized upside-down apple tart
Tendron	Veal or beef rib
Terrine	Baked minced meat or fish
Thé	Tea
Thon	Tuna
Thym	Thyme
Tian	Provençal vegetable casserole
Tiède	Lukewarm
Topinambour	Jerusalem artichoke
Tournedos	Fillet steak
Tourte	Covered savoury tart
Tourteau	Large crab

Travers de porc	Spare ribs
Tripes	Tripe
Truffe	Truffle
Truite	Trout
Turbot(in)	(Small) turbot
Vacherin	Meringue ring filled with whipped cream, ice-cream and fruit
Vallée d'Auge	With Calvados, apples and cream
Vanille	Vanilla
Vapeur (à la)	Steamed
Veau	Veal
- pané	- breadcrumbed escalope
- à la Viennoise	- escalope with chopped egg, capers and parsley
Velouté	Cream sauce / soup
Venaison	Venison
Vénus	Tiny clam
Verjus	Juice of unripe grapes
Verveine	Lemon verbena herb tea
Viande	Meat
Vinaigre	Vinegar
Vinaigre de framboise	Raspberry vinegar
Vinaigre de xérès	Sherry vinegar
Vinaigrette	Oil and vinegar dressing
Vivier	Fish tank (in restaurant)
Volaille	Poultry
Vol-au-vent	Puff pastry shell
Yaourt	Yogurt
Zeste	Orange and lemon peel (coloured part only)

145

Smoking

Smoking is no longer allowed in public places, cafés, restaurants etc. in France. There are often spaces for smokers in restaurants and cafés however!

(Once again illustrating the triumph of French individualism over officialdom, of pragmatism over idealism!)

Tipping

This is a widespread practice. In general, the following guidelines apply:

- **Taxis** 10-15% of meter charge.
- **Porters** 5F in addition to set charges
- **Toilet / petrol pump attendants** 2F
- **Waiters** 15-20%
- **Guides** 10-15%
- **Usherettes** 5F
- **Hairdressers** 10-15%

Where service charges apply, it is still customary to leave some small change for the waiter.

DO NOT forget to tip usherettes / theatre staff as you are likely to provoke a very vocal response in front of the whole audience!

It is also vital to leave a tip for the lavatory attendant! It is not unknown for customers to be pursued into the street if they fail to do so! (There are woman attendants in both sexes' toilets).

"Champions of France"
Rules of Boules

- The game is played by two teams of two or three players. In teams of two (**doublettes**) each player has three **boules**; in teams of three (**triplettes**) each player has two **boules**.

- Players use metal **boules**, diameter between 7cm and 8cm, weight not to exceed 800 gms.

- The marker ball (**cochonnet**) is wooden, diameter between 25cm and 30cm.

- The starter team is decided by toss of a coin. One member of the team chooses the starting place and draws on the ground a circle in which to stand, 36cm to 50cm across. Both feet of the player must remain inside the circle until the **boule** lands.

- The first thrower throws the **cochonnet** between 6m and 10m away, not nearer than 50cm from any obstacle (wall, tree etc).

- A player in the other team then comes into the circle and tries to throw his boule nearer to the **cochonnet**, or knock away the leading **boule**. The boule nearest to the **cochonnet** leads.

- Then it is up to a player in the team not leading to throw until his team gets a leading **boule**, and so on ...

- When a team has no more **boules** the players of   the other team throw theirs and try to place them as close as possible to the **cochonnet.**

- When both teams have no more **boules** the points are counted. The winning team gets as many points as it has **boules** nearer than the best of the losing team.

- A player of the winning team throws the **cochonnet** from where it is, and the game starts again until one team reaches 13 points.

8

Money matters!

Banking

Banks are open from 9am to 12 noon and 2 to 4pm and are usually closed on Saturday; some branches have limited operations on Saturday but will close on Monday.

Travellers' Cheques can be cashed at banks or **bureaux de change** at airports, terminals and the larger railway stations and in some hotels and shops. A passport is required when cashing cheques in banks. Commission charges vary and hotels usually charge more than banks for cashing cheques. Most banks have cash dispensers which accept international credit cards. Difficulties are still reported with **Crédit Agricole** dispensers in some areas since they may refuse to accept foreign cards.

Beware of the custom of closing on and around public holidays. For example, if a public holiday falls on a Thursday, the bank will **faire le pont**, that is bridge the gap by closing on the Friday as well. In some small towns, the bank opens only on Market Days! In Nageac, for example, the branch of one well-known bank opens for one hour every Tuesday afternoon, and this is a tourist area! In some tourist areas, times will be different in the Low Season.

Credit Cards

American Express, **Carte Bleue** (Visa / Barclaycard), Diners Club and Eurocard (Mastercard) are widely accepted in shops, hotels, restaurants and petrol stations. Progressively fewer establishments will accept Eurocheques, even backed by the Eurocheque card. Those that do may levy hefty surcharges, allegedly to cover administrative charges by their own Bank. Do ask before committing yourself! In 1996, British banks warned their customers travelling in France to be aware that the Eurocheque Encashment Service was, they gathered, apparently not being honoured by most French banks and the **Poste (PTT)**. Cash can still be obtained from ATMs using the EU Card. There are over 15,800 of these cash machines, but they tend to run out of cash by Sunday!

French bank cards are of the "smart" variety which does not incorporate the old-fashioned magnetic strip. French shoppers are handed a key pad at the till on which they enter their PIN number. Foreign cards do not require such validation and one should not (in theory, at least) be asked for it. British banks are now notifying their customers that if keypad validation is required for credit cards, the UK PIN will work. All establishments are legally obliged to accept British and other foreign style cards, but many restaurants, filling stations and shops are now refusing them.

The French Government Tourist Office has proposed a phrase to be used in these circumstances in the event of a resounding **NON!** -

> **"Ma carte n'est pas une carte à puce, mais à piste magnétique. Elle est valable et je vous serais reconnaissant d'en demander la confirmation auprès de votre banque ou de votre centre de traitement".**
>
> (My card is not of the smart variety, but has a magnetic strip. It is valid and I would be grateful if you could check its validity with your bank or clearing centre).

Some shops and hypermarkets have a minimum spending amount and may also require ID with a photo such as a passport

A European Debit Card, issued by the major UK Banks is usable like Switch and requires your PIN to be entered at the point of sale. Look for the symbol

REMEMBER: Combined Card Accounts e.g. Mastercard / Visa will both be cancelled if the loss of one card is reported. You will be left cardless! The banks do not advertise this fact as a selling point! Similarly, cards issued to joint account holders will all be cancelled.

Be aware too that automatic 24 hour pumps at filling stations may not accept foreign cards. Check before filling up also at self-serve stations that your card will be acceptable. Just because you used it at one branch of a particular **Grande Surface** does not mean that it will be usable at all branches of the same company!

Bank

ATM (Cash machine)	Retrait de Billets
bank card	carte bancaire / bleue fs
blank cheque	chèque en blanc ms
can I buy travellers' cheques here?	puis-je acheter des chèques de voyage ici?
can I have them now or shall I come back?	vous pouvez me les donner tout de suite ou dois-je repasser?
can I have small denominations?	vous pouvez me faire des petites coupures svp?

can I withdraw money on Mastercard?	puis-je utiliser ma carte Mastercard pour retirer de l'argent?
can you give me small notes?	vous pouvez me donner des petits billets?
cheque for ... FF	un chèque d'un montant de FF ...
could you change this note?	puis-je avoir de la monnaie pour ce billet?
credit card	carte de crédit fs
do I have to go to the cashier?	je dois passer à la caisse?
do you want proof of identity?	voulez-vous une pièce d'identité?
draw a cheque	tirer un chèque
foreign coins	des espèces étrangères
from my account in Britain	de mon compte en Grande Bretagne
here is my ID	voici ma pièce d'identité
here is the authorisation for ...	voici le pouvoir pour ...
I have an account at the ... Bank	j'ai un compte à la Banque de ...
I have endorsed the cheque	j'ai bien endossé le chèque
I have lost my cheque book	j'ai perdu mon carnet de chèques
I want to arrange a transfer	je voudrais arranger un virement
I would like some foreign currency	je voudrais des devises étrangères
I would like to change my French money	je voudrais changer mon argent français
I'd like to cash this travellers' cheque	je voudrais toucher ce chèque de voyage
I'd like to withdraw 1000F in cash	je voudrais retirer mille francs en liquide
in 200F notes	en coupures de deux cents francs

in cash	en liquide
is there a 24hr machine?	y a-t-il un guichet automatique?
make out a cheque	libeller un chèque
pay cash	payer comptant
pay in advance	payer d'avance
pay, settle	régler
remit	verser, virer

the exchange rate	cours du change ms
to debit	débiter
to whom should I give it?	à qui faut-il la remettre?
transfer	transférer
transfer authority	ordre de transfert ms
what is the exchange rate today?	quel est le cours du change aujourd'hui?
what is the rate for the pound today?	la livre vaut combien aujourd'hui?
where do I sign?	je signe où?

Shopping

Sales take place twice a year, in January and July - in theory at least! They cannot exceed a two month period. A sales item must bear a label showing the former price crossed out and the sales price. If two identical articles are priced differently, you can ask to pay the lower price, provided it corresponds to the value. Do not hesitate to refuse to pay a price that is different from the marked price.

Giving the wrong change to foreigners who appear not to speak the language is, sadly, somewhat of an art form in France. Be wary, especially in tourist areas and airports! A favourite trick on trains is for the bar and restaurant staff not to have change "until the end of the journey". They then disappear and proof, if you dare to complain to officialdom, is virtually impossible! Anyone who allows himself to be caught is considered stupid and legitimate game.

For large purchases, an order form is required. There are two types of deposits: "**arrhes**" and "**acompte**". The former allows you to cancel the order but lose the deposit. The latter does not allow cancellation. If the shopkeeper breaks the contract he must pay you twice the amount.

With door-to-door selling and credit there is a cooling-off period of 7 days. This does not apply to purchases made at a show or fair. Credit notes are at the discretion of the shopkeeper if you have changed your mind.

Warranties in France are limited to 6 or 12 months on consumer goods and may not be valid abroad, even in other EU countries.

A bill must be provided for all purchases over 100FF. (See also Taxis)

A frequent source of confusion is the reversal in the use of the comma and decimal point in sums of money and numbers in general. Thus 1.500 in France is 1,500 whereas 1,50 is 1.50 This has been changing as the influence of digital shop tills and calculators spreads. Care is needed, especially when pricing items or checking credit card slips for example, to avoid unpleasant and expensive shocks. A British restaurant customer recently paid £2000 by credit card for an omelette in France!

Beware also of the handwritten number 1. It can be very similar to the British 7.

A very strange French quirk of which one must be aware, is the common tendency to refer to sums of money in terms of **Centimes**! This is done only with large amounts such as are involved in car or house purchase, but the point at which Francs become **centimes** is, it seems, "**au choix**". Thus "**un million**" (**de centimes**) would mean "**cent mille francs**"! Often when the French mention large sums, they have to specify even to each other whether they mean **centimes** or **francs**. To compound the confusion for the uninitiated and bemused foreigner, the term "**nouveaux Francs**" (**NF**) is also sometimes used, despite the fact that the current Franc was born in 1959, before some of the people who use the expression were themselves born! "**Francs durs**" is also heard! However you are not likely to come across them in the local market. You will though encounter the "**livre**" or pound weight, which is not really a pound but half a kilo. This officially disappeared at the beginning of the 19th century when metrication was introduced. Traditions die hard! It remains to be seen what will happen with the Euro!

The main hyper / supermarkets are Auchan, Casino, Champion, Continent, Intermarché, Leclerc and Super U. Smaller supermarkets are Timy, Huit à 8 and Spar.

- Remember that it is considered good manners to say "**Bonjour Messieurs / Dames**" when you enter a bank, small shop etc where there are not many people. This is particularly true of villages and provincial towns.

- A useful service in some stores is the self scan machine to check prices where these are not marked.

- Fruit and vegetables often have to be weighed by the customer. You place the goods on the scale, press the appropriate picture symbol and a label is printed which you then stick on the plastic bag.

- Some hypermarkets such as Auchan require you either to deposit your shopping bag at a special desk before you enter, or shrinkwrap it. This "Ensachage" may be self-service .

- In some establishments, look out for the till reserved for holders of store cards, "Caisse Réservée. You can save yourself time and embarrassment if you avoid it.

- Most Hypermarkets require you to leave through a special exit if you have made no purchases - "**Sortie Sans Achat**".

- Pregnant women have a special checkout at Auchan - **Future Maman**

Conversion Factors

Weights and Measures

Gallons >	Litres	(x 4.55)
Litres >	Gallons	(÷ 4.55)
Lbs >	Kilos	(÷ 2.2)
Kilos >	Lbs	(x 2.2)
Miles >	Kms	(÷ 0.625)
Kms >	Miles	(x 0.625)
Feet >	Metres	(x 0.3)
Metres >	Feet	(÷ 0.3)

Temperatures

F > C   (-32 then x 0.56)

C > F   (x 1.8 then +32)

Map Scales / Rough Equivalent

Map Scales	Rough Equivalent
1:15000	0.25 mile to inch
1:25000	1 mile to 2.5 inch
1:50000	1 mile to 1 inch
1:100000	1.75 miles to 1 inch
1:200000	3.25 miles to 1 inch
1:250000	4 miles to 1 inch

Tyre Pressures

PSI > Bar (x 0.07)
Bar > PSI (÷ 0.07)

Mile	Kilometres	Miles	Kilometres
1	1.6	30	48.3
2	3.2	40	64.4
3	4.8	50	80.5
4	6.4	60	96.6
5	8.1	70	112.7
6	9.7	80	128.7
7	11.3	90	144.8
8	12.9	100	160.9
9	14.5	200	321.9
10	16.1	300	482.8
15	24.1	400	643.7
20	32.2	500	804.7

Gallons	Litres	Litres	Gallons
1	4.55	1	0.22
2	9.09	5	1.10
3	13.64	20	4.40
4	18.18	30	6.60
5	22.73	50	11.00
10	45.46	75	16.50
15	68.19	100	22.00

PSI	Kg/Cm2/Bar
18	1.27
20	1.41
22	1.55
24	1.69
26	1.83
28	1.97
30	2.11
32	2.25
34	2.39
36	2.53
38	2.67
40	2.81

Shopping: clothes

Women's clothes

UK	10	10	12	14	16	18	20	22
Continental	36	38	40	42	44	46	48	50

Women's shoes

UK	3	4	5	6	7	8
Continental	35	36	37	38	39	40

Men's clothes							
UK	36	38	40	42	44	46	48
Continental	46	48	50	52	54	56	58

Men's shirts								
UK	14	14.5	15	15.5	16	16.5	17	17.5
Continental	36	37	38	39	40	41	42	43

Men's Shoes							
UK	5	6	7	8	9	10	11
Continental	39	40	41	42	43	44	45

Shopping

Some useful words and phrases

browsers welcome	entrée libre fs
could you pass me ... ?	vous pouvez me passer ... ?
could you help me?	pourriez-vous m'aider?
could you show me ... ?	pourriez-vous me montrer ... ?
have you ... ?	avez-vous ... ?
herbalist	herboristerie fs
I am only looking	je ne fais que regarder
I wonder if you have ... ?	auriez-vous ... ?
I'd like ...	je voudrais ...
I'd like to see the ... in the window	je voudrais voir le / la ... qui est en vitrine
in the window / on display	en vitrine / à l'étalage
leather goods	maroquinerie fs
some models are not on show	certains modèles ne sont pas présentés
thank you, I am being served	merci, on s'occupe de moi
the one in the window display	celui (m) / celle (f) qui est en vitrine / à l'étalage
watch repairer's	horlogerie fs
where do I pay?	où est la caisse?
where is the ... department?	où se trouve le rayon ... ?
where is the lift?	où est l'ascenseur?

Perhaps you would like something different from what you are shown:

eg   Have you something bigger?

      Avez-vous quelque chose de plus grand?

or

de plus ...

lower	bas
dearer	cher
lighter	clair
thicker	épais
darker	foncé
higher, taller	haut
prettier	joli
heavier	lourd
thinner	mince
thinner	petit
sturdier	solide

In a different material:

have you got one in ...

l'avez-vous en ... ?

bronze	bronze
cast iron	fonte
cotton	coton
gold	or
lace	dentelle
leather	cuir
metal	métal
nylon	nylon
plastic	plastique
satin	satin
silk	soie
silver	argent
suede	daim
velvet	velours
wood	bois

or:

can you order it / them for me?	pourriez-vous me le / la / les commander?
have you anything better?	avez-vous quelque chose de meilleur?
have you anything cheaper?	avez-vous quelque chose de meilleur marché?
how long will it take?	combien de temps cela prendra-t-il?
I don't want anything too dear	je ne voudrais pas quelque chose de trop cher
I don't want to spend more than ...	je ne veux pas dépenser plus de ... francs
it isn't quite what I want	ce n'est pas exactement ce que je veux
no, I don't like it	non, cela ne me plaît pas

I would like a ... one
je voudrais un ...

big	grand
blue	bleu
cheap	bon marché
dark	foncé
good	bon
green	vert
grey	gris
heavy	lourd
light	léger
oval	ovale
pink	rose
rectangular	rectangulaire
red	rouge
round	rond
small	petit
square	carré
sturdy	solide
white	blanc
yellow	jaune

5 articles only	5 articles maxi
are you being served?	on vous sert?
can I bring it back for a refund?	puis-je le / la rapporter pour me faire rembourser?
by length or by the roll?	à la découpe ou au rouleau?
by Saturday?	pour samedi?
can I bleach it?	puis-je le / la blanchir?
can I bring it back for a refund?	puis-je le / la rapporter pour me faire rembourser?
can I dye it?	puis-je le / la teindre?
can I hand wash it / them?	puis-je le / la / les laver à la main?

can I pay by Mastercard / Visa / credit card?	puis-je payer par Mastercard / Visa / carte de crédit?
can you alter it for me?	vous pouvez me le / la retoucher?
can you deliver it / them?	pouvez-vous le / la / les livrer?

can you gift-wrap it for me?	vous pouvez me faire un paquet-cadeau?
can you wrap it for me?	vous pouvez me l'envelopper?
could you carry it / them to my car?	pourriez-vous le / la / les porter à ma voiture?
could you measure me?	pouvez-vous prendre mes mesures?
do I have to come back or wait?	je dois repasser où attendre?
do I have to wash it / them separately?	faut-il le / la / les laver séparément?
do you close for lunch?	fermez-vous à midi?
do you do credit terms?	il y a des facilités de paiement?
do you do quantity discounts?	vous faites des remises pour les grosses quantités?
do you sell ... at reduced prices?	vous vendez les ... au rabais?
do you sell it by the length?	le / la vendez-vous à la découpe?
do you sell it cut to order? (food)	le / la vendez-vous à la coupe?
do you sell it in bulk / loose?	vous le vendez en vrac?
do you sell it wholesale / retail?	vous le / la vendez en gros / au détail?
do you sell spares for ... ?	vendez-vous les pièces détachées pour ... ?
do you stay open all day?	faites-vous la journée continue?
do you sell tights?	vendez-vous les collants?
do you take Eurocheques?	acceptez-vous les Eurochèques?
do you take off the discount at the till?	vous me faites l'escompte de caisse?
do you take travellers' cheques?	acceptez-vous les chèques de voyage?
does it / do they have to be dry cleaned?	faut-il le / la / les faire nettoyer à sec?
does it suit me?	cela me va-t-il / elle?
Exit without purchases	Sortie sans Achat
Fast Checkout	Caisse Rapide

give me 10 francs worth	donnez-m'en pour 10 francs
give me large / middling / small ones	donnez-moi des grosses / moyennes / petites
give me some ten franc coins	donnez-moi des pièces de 10 francs
have you a cardboard box?	auriez-vous une boîte en carton?
have you a film for this camera?	avez-vous une pellicule pour cet appareil?
have you a mirror?	vous avez un miroir?
have you a refill?	auriez-vous une recharge?
have you got change for 50 francs?	avez-vous la monnaie de / sur 50 francs?
have you kept your Visa receipt ?	vous auriez peut-être gardé la facturette Visa?
have you something more / less ... ?	avez-vous quelque chose de plus / moins ... ?
how do you sell it / them?	vous le / la / les vendez comment?
how long does it take to ... ?	combien de temps faut-il compter pour ... ?
how much are they each?	c'est combien la pièce?
how much do I owe you?	je vous dois combien?
how much does it come to?	cela fait combien?
how much is it per kilo / mètre?	c'est combien le kilo / le mètre?
how much is it?	c'est combien?
I gave you a 100 franc note	je vous ai donné un billet de cent francs
I have other shopping to do	j'ai d'autres commissions à faire
I need a 36	il me faut du trente-six
I need a spare ...	il me faut un / une ... de rechange
I take a 42	je porte du 42

I'd like a pound / half kilo of ...	je voudrais une livre / un demi-kilo de …
I'd like a top to go with this skirt	je voudrais un haut qui aille avec cette jupe
if it doesn't suit me may I bring it / them back?	si cela ne me va pas puis-je le / la / les rapporter?
I'll take it / them	je le / la / les prends
I'll take it with me	je l'emporte
I'll take this one instead	je prends plutôt celui / celle-ci
I'll think about it	je vais y réfléchir

I'll try the ... instead	j'essayerai plutôt ...
I'm sorry, I haven't any change	je m'excuse, je n'ai pas de monnaie
in stock	en stock
in the bill	dans la note
in what name?	à quel nom?
is it a genuine ... ?	c'est un / une ... véritable ... ?
is it a gift?	c'est pour offrir?
is it crease resistant?	c'est infroissable?
is it drip dry?	c'est lavé-repassé?
is it the only pattern you have in stock?	est-ce le seul modèle que vous ayez en magasin?
is it the sale price?	c'est le prix de solde?
is there a charge?	y a-t-il un supplément?
is there a special treatment for this leather?	y a-t-il un traitement spécial pour ce cuir?
is there anything else?	et avec ça?
is this the only quality / size?	est-ce là la seule qualité / la seule taille?
it doesn't suit me	cela ne me va pas
it is quite / too dear	c'est assez / trop cher
it is too long / small / dear / loose / short	c'est trop long / petit / cher / large / court
it suits me perfectly	ça va à la perfection / à merveille
it's just what I need	c'est juste ce qu'il me faut
matching	assorti
may I have a bag please?	puis-je avoir un sac svp?
may I have a plastic bag?	puis-je avoir une pochette en plastique?
may I leave it / them here?	puis-je le / la / les laisser ici?
may I try it (on)?	puis-je l'essayer?
no thank you, that will be all	non merci, ce sera tout
nothing else	rien de plus
please post it to this address	veuillez me l'expédier par la poste
please put it right	veuillez la rectifier
please wrap it	veuillez l'envelopper
shall I make out a cheque?	je vous fais un chèque?
thanks anyway	merci beaucoup quand même
that's all, thank you	c'est tout merci
the bill please	la note svp
there is no label, where is it made?	il n'y a pas d'étiquette, il / elle est fabriqué(e) où?
there would appear to be a mistake	il me semble qu'il y a une erreur
this is not suitable	ceci ne fait pas l'affaire
this will do	ceci fait l'affaire
till closed	caisse fermée
to whom shall I make it payable?	je le libelle à quel nom?
twenty francs worth of ...	pour 20 francs de ...

we are out of stock of ...	les ... manquent en magasin
what is your lowest price?	quel est votre dernier prix?
what time do you close?	à quelle heure fermez-vous?
what time does the shop open?	le magasin est ouvert à partir de quelle heure?
when will you be able to do it for?	pour quand pouvez-vous le faire?
where is the fitting cubicle?	où est la cabine d'essayage?
will it fade?	cela va se décolorer?
will it shrink?	c'est irrétrécissable?
will the colour run?	est-ce que le tissu va se déteindre?
will you give me a receipt?	vous me donnez un reçu?

Complaining / Exchanging / Problems

> **Consumer problems: Free Number 0800 12 05 12 (July and August only)**

can I exchange it?	puis-je l'échanger?
can you change it?	pouvez-vous la changer?
can you reduce this article?	pouvez-vous baisser le prix?
can you repair it / them for me?	pouvez-vous me le / la / les réparer?
could you give me a refund?	vous ne pourriez pas me rembourser?
could you recharge it for me?	pourriez-vous me la recharger?
do you sell unusual sizes?	vendez-vous les tailles exceptionnelles / spéciales / non-courantes / hors-série?
go to the central cash desk	adressez-vous à la caisse centrale
have you a bigger / smaller size?	l'avez-vous dans une taille plus grande / petite?
have you another branch where I might get one?	avez-vous une autre branche où je pourrais en obtenir un?
have you another one like this?	en avez-vous un / une autre comme celui- / celle-ci?
have you anything more sturdy / reliable	vous n'auriez pas quelque chose de plus solide

here is my receipt	voici ma quittance / voici mon reçu
here is the warranty	voici le bon de garantie
how much current does it draw?	ça tire combien d'ampères?
I am not at all satisfied with the quality	je ne suis pas du tout satisfait(e) de la qualité
I bought it yesterday / the day before yesterday	je l'ai acheté hier / avant-hier
I bought too many	j'en ai acheté de trop
I can't find ...	je ne trouve pas ...
I need something which runs off batteries	il m'en faut un qui s'alimente sur piles
I was wrong about my size (shoes, gloves)	je me suis trompé(e) de taille / (clothes) de pointure
I'd like a credit note please	je voudrais une note de crédit svp
I'd like a refund	je voudrais me faire rembourser
I'd like to return this	je voudrais vous rendre ceci
if I find that it is not what I need ...	si éventuellement je trouve que ce n'est pas qu'il me faut ...
it caused a short-circuit	ça a causé un court-circuit
it has a very unpleasant taste	ça a un très mauvais goût
it has buckled	cela a gondolé
it is a bit tight round the hips / under the arms	il / elle me serre un peu trop aux hanches / sous les bras
it is a little tight	il / elle est un peu étroit(e)
it is dirty / torn	c'est sale / déchiré
it is not ... enough	il n'est pas assez ...
it is not waterproof	ce n'est pas imperméable (clothes)
it is not watertight	ce n'est pas étanche
it is scratched	c'est égratigné / rayé
it is the young woman over there who served me	c'est mademoiselle là-bas qui m'a servi
it worked alright at first	cela a fonctionné comme il fallait au début
large sizes	les grandes tailles
may I bring it back for a refund?	puis-je le / la rapporter pour me faire rembourser?
may I compare the colours in daylight?	puis-je comparer les couleurs à la lumière du jour?
may I go as far as the door?	puis-je aller jusqu'à la porte?
my 10F coin is stuck in the machine / trolley	ma pièce de 10 francs est coincée dans la machine / le caddy
small sizes	les petites tailles
the batteries are flat	les piles sont à plat
the case is damaged	la boîte est endommagée
the lift is out of order	l'ascenseur ne marche pas
the neckline is too low	il / elle est trop décolleté(e)
the pair do not match	les deux ne vont pas ensemble
the seal is broken	le cachet est cassé
the zip is jammed	la fermeture est bloquée

there are cracks	il y a des fêlures (wood) / brisures / fentes (metal)
the bulb has blown	l'ampoule est grillée
there are flaws	il y a des imperfections / défauts
there is a bottle missing in this pack	il manque une bouteille dans ce pack
there is a little tear, here	il y a une petite déchirure, là
there is a loose wire	il y a un fil détaché
there is too much play	il y a trop de jeu
there was a smell of burning	ça sentait le brûlé
these ... are not right	ces ... ne sont pas comme il faut
these stockings do not match	ces bas ne vont pas ensemble
this ... does not work	ce / cette ... ne marche pas
this ... is broken	ce / cette ... est cassé(e)
this ... is not the right colour	ce / cette ... n'est pas de la couleur qu'il me fallait
this ... is stale ("off")	ce / cette ... n'est plus frais / fraîche
this battery is flat	cette batterie est à plat
this beer is flat	cette bière est éventée
this bottle / can / container leaks	cette bouteille / canette / ce bidon fuit
this dress is faded	cette robe est passée
this equipment only works on mains	cet appareil ne marche que sur secteur
this meat is off	cette viande est avancée
this record is faulty	ce disque est défectueux
this sweater is too big	ce pull est trop grand
this watch gains / loses ten minutes	cette montre avance / retarde de dix minutes
unfortunately I have lost the receipt	malheureusement j'ai égaré le reçu
very large sizes (men)	les très grands patrons
well made / reliable	solide / fiable
what I need	ce qu'il me faut
what size fuse do I need?	il me faut un plomb de quelle valeur?
when I dropped it on the floor	quand je l'ai laissé tomber par terre
when I switched it on, the fuse blew	quand je l'ai branché, le plomb a sauté
where do I have to go to exchange something?	où faut-il s'adresser pour échanger quelque chose?
will you exchange it for me?	vous pouvez me la changer?
you gave me change for 50 francs	vous m'avez rendu la monnaie de 50F
you have given me the wrong change	vous ne m'avez pas assez rendu assez
you have rung up something I have not bought	vous avez pointé quelque chose que je n'ai pas acheté
you should have asked at the desk over there	il fallait demander au bureau là-bas
you should have told me	vous auriez dû me le dire

Hairdressing

bleach	décoloration fs
blow dry	brushing ms
can I blow dry it?	puis-je les faire sécher au sèche-cheveux?
can I have a perm?	puis-je me faire faire une mise en plis?
can I have an appointment for ... ?	puis-je prendre rendez-vous pour ... ?
colour rinse	coloration fs
could you cut off a little more here?	voulez-vous bien couper un peu plus ici?
could you trim my ...	pourriez-vous me rafraîchir les ...
do not use hairspray	n'utilisez pas de laque
dye	teinture fs
have you a colour chart?	avez-vous un nuancier?
have you a mirror?	vous avez une glace svp?
how long will it take?	j'en aurai pour combien de temps?
I don't want an apprentice	je ne veux pas d'apprenti
I don't want any hairspray	je ne veux pas de laque
I have bleached hair	j'ai les cheveux oxygénés
I'd like a conditioner	mettez-moi une lotion capillaire
I'd like a darker / lighter shade	je voudrais une teinte plus foncée / plus claire
I'd like a haircut please	coupe de cheveux svp fs
I'd like a manicure	je voudrais un manucure
I'd like a perm	je voudrais me faire faire une permanente
I'd like a re-style	je voudrais une nouvelle coiffure
I'd like a rinse	je voudrais un rinçage
I'd like a shampoo	je voudrais un shampooing
I'd like a trim	je voudrais me faire faire une coupe d'entretien
I'd like an appointment for ...	je voudrais un rendez-vous pour ...
I'd like it cut and shaped	je voudrais une coupe et une mise en plis

I'd like to make an appointment for	je voudrais un rendez-vous pour
Monday morning	lundi matin
I'd like my hair highlighted	je voudrais me faire faire des reflets
I'd like to see a colour chart	je voudrais voir la gamme des coloris
I would like a normal cut	je voudrais une coupe ordinaire
in front	par devant
it seems a little uneven	il me semble que ça manque un peu de symétrie
may I see some fashion magazines	puis-je regarder des journaux de modes?
my beard / moustache / sideboards	ma barbe / ma moustache / mes favoris
neck / sides / back	nuque fs / côtés mpl / derrière
normal / dry / greasy	cheveux normaux / secs / gras
not too short at the sides	pas trop courts sur le côté
not too short please	pas trop court svp
setting lotion	fixatif ms
short at the back	courts par derrière
shorter at the back	je les voudrais un peu plus courts derrière
the dryer is too hot	le séchoir est trop chaud
the top	haut de la tête ms
the water is too cold	l'eau est trop froide
will I be able to buy this product in the shops?	je pourrai acheter ce produit dans les magasins?
will it be easy to look after?	ce sera facile à entretenir?
with a fringe	avec une frange

9

And Finally ...

 **France Telecom**

Public Telephones

- French coin operated payphones are quite rare nowadays. Card phones are however located throughout the country in public places (on the street, railway stations, airports etc ...).

- 50 or 120 "**Unités Télécom**" cards called "**Télécarte**" are available for use in card operated phones. They can be purchased at tobacconists, post offices, newsagents, wherever you see the "**TELECARTE EN VENTE ICI**" sign (authorised suppliers), and in agencies.

- Card vending machines are available in some newer public buildings such as Ferry Terminals.

- Cards are usable for both national and international calls.

- Not all telephone boxes in France can be called. Those that can are sometimes marked with a blue bell symbol.

- Emergency Calls are free and do not require the initial use of a coin or card as in some countries.

- Some phones do not return unused coins - **Cet appareil ne rend pas la monnaie**

Telephone Calls within France

All of France is now divided into 5 numbered zones, requiring a prefix before the subscriber's number as shown on this map :

If you wish to call a French subscriber but have only the **old** number, you must dial the **two relevant digits** before it. These will vary according to the location as shown. Precise details are listed in callboxes.

```
                        Call Box Instructions
Cards:

Décrochez                               Lift Receiver

Introduire Carte ou Faire Numéro Libre  Insert card or dial free number

Patientez SVP                           Wait please

Crédit 6 Unités                         Number of units left

Retirez Votre Carte                     Take Card

Raccrochez                              Replace receiver
```

Some public telephones take credit cards but they are only found in large airports, railway stations, international hotels and the like. There is a choice of language.

```
The instructions are as follows:

                        Décrochez          Lift receiver

                        Choisir sa langue  Choose language

                        Introduire la carte Insert Card

                        Numérotez          Dial number
```

Telephone   Callbands

A   Monday-Friday
B   Saturday
C   Sunday

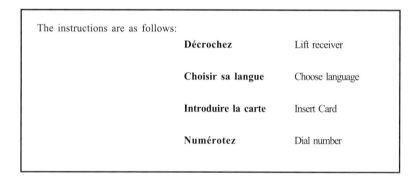

French **Publiphones** sometimes do not recognise their own cards! When the LCD screen shows

167

'anomalie retirez SVP' or a similar message, persist until it gives in and allows you to use your card! Several insertions are usually sufficient. Sometimes the message is **"cette carte n'est pas valable"** - "This card is not valid". When it is working properly, there will be the message:

"crédit X unités"- "X units left". **"Numérotez"** ie "Dial your number".
or
"suivre les indications de l'écran de lecture" - "Follow screen instructions".

Telephoning abroad

Using the telephone in an hotel room and sometimes on a campsite (unless in a public callbox) will incur very heavy charges. It is always best to use a kiosk or direct dialling facility unless this is not possible.

Overseas enquiries
Tel: 00 33 12 44   UK Directory Enquiries.

- When dialling the UK from France, omit the zero of the exchange code.eg when dialling Southampton (Code 01703) Dial 00 44 1703 + Subscriber's Number.

- Since most subscribers now use the Minitel to find telephone numbers, directories tend to be scarce and out of date.

- Minitel terminals are available in post offices. They are free and easy to use.

1	Press "Prise de Ligne" key
2	Type 3611 and wait for the beep
3	Press "Connexion-Fin"
4	Follow the screen instructions to find the subscriber's number. These are fairly obvious.

At busy times you may hear the following message:

"En raison de l'encombrement des lignes, votre communication ne peut pas aboutir. Veuillez appeler ultérieurement"
"All lines are busy. Your call cannot be put through. Please try again later".

Unobtainable numbers are indicated by the following message:

"Le numéro que vous avez appelé n'a pas été attribué".
"The number you have called has not been recognized".

Out and About

are there any classical music concerts?	y a-t-il des concerts de musique classique?
are there any coach trips?	y a-t-il des excursions en car?
are there any guided tours?	y a-t-il des visites guidées?
are there any local walks?	y a-t-il des sentiers de petite randonnée?
are there reduced rates during the week?	y a-t-il des tarifs réduits en semaine?
can one book by telephone?	peut-on réserver par téléphone?
can one visit the chateau?	le château, est-il visitable?
can one visit?	on peut visiter / peut-on visiter?
can you reserve me a room?	pouvez-vous me réserver une chambre?
does not close for lunch	ouvert en permanence
free entrance	visite gratuite fs
have you a guide to local walks?	avez-vous un guide des petites randonnées?
have you a list of car hire firms?	avez-vous une liste des agences de location de voitures?
have you a list of restaurants?	avez-vous une liste des restaurants?
have you a plan of the town	avez-vous un plan de la ville?
have you the train / bus timetables for ... ?	avez-vous les horaires des trains / bus pour ... ?
I would like some information	je voudrais des renseignements
is an appointment necessary?	faut-il prendre rendez-vous?
is entry free or is there a charge?	l'entrée est gratuite ou payante?
is there a cinema / theatre in town?	y a-t-il un cinéma / théâtre en ville?
lamb roasting	un méchoui
light and sound	son et lumière ms
list of hotels	une liste des hôtels
map of the bus routes	un plan du réseau routier
place of historical interest	monument historique ms
plan of the rail network	un plan du réseau ferroviaire?
programme of summer events / concerts	un calendrier des manifestations / concerts d'été
Sundays are free	le dimanche c'est gratuit
the local bus / train timetables	les horaires des bus / des trains locaux

tourist itinerary (on foot)	sentier de découverte
unaccompanied visit	visite libre fs
what are the opening hours?	quelles sont les heures de visite?
what are the opening times?	quelles en sont les heures d'ouverture?
what days is it open?	quelles sont les jours ouvrables?
what time of the year does the Jazz Festival take place?	le Festival de Jazz a lieu à quelle époque?
what's on at the moment?	qu'est-ce qu'on donne en ce moment?
when is market day?	quel est le jour du marché?
where can one reserve theatre tickets?	où peut-on réserver des places de théâtre?
which day is it closed?	quel est le jour de fermeture?

Sanisettes (Automatic toilets)

Beware of the Automatic type of street toilet if you have very small children. It works on the weight of the occupant and can malfunction. The flush and clean cycle involves the whole pedestal tipping upside down for mechanical scrubbing and several children have been killed, some ending up in the sewers, because the system assumed that the occupant had left. An adult should always accompany a very small child. Be aware too that there is a time limit - you could end up on view!

National Holidays

Jan 1
Easter Monday
May 1
May 8
Ascension
Pentecost
Jul 14
Aug 15
Nov 1
Nov 11
Dec 25

Post Office

LA POSTE

50 / 120 unit Phone Card	une télécarte à 50 unités / à 120 unités
a book of stamps	un carnet de timbres tarif normal
a stamp for this please	un timbre pour ceci svp
abroad	étranger
by airmail	par avion
collection time	heure de la levée fs
deliveries	livraisons fpl
do I have to make a Customs Declaration?	faut-il faire une Déclaration de Douane?
First Class letter to an EU country	une lettre à tarif normal pour la CEE
have I missed the last collection?	ai-je raté la dernière levée?
have you any mail for me?	avez-vous du courrier pour moi?
have you the Var phone directory?	avez-vous l'annuaire téléphone pour le Var?
I'd like 10 First / Second class stamps	je voudrais 10 timbres, tarif normal / réduit
I'd like a postal order	je voudrais un mandat-poste

I'd like to send a fax	je voudrais faire envoyer une télécopie
I'd like to send this letter to ...	je voudrais envoyer cette lettre en ...
other destinations	autres destinations fpl
Poste Restante	poste-restante fs
Recorded Delivery	avec accusé de réception ms
six stamps for post cards	six timbres pour cartes postales
stamp machine	distributeur de timbres ms
surface mail	courrier ordinaire ms
what is the postage for this letter to G-B?	quel est le port pour cette lettre pour la G-B?
what is the postage to ... ?	quel est l'affranchissement pour ... ?
what time is the first / last collection?	la première / dernière levée est à quelle heure?

Tobacconists sell stamps too.

Whatever your mode of transport, tow vehicle or accommodation,
Bonnes vacances!

Index

175

176